TORI KRUSE

MISS MISSOURI USA

UNEXPECTED
HOW TO PERSEVERE BEYOND YOUR LIMITS

Unexpected: How to Persevere Beyond Your Limits

© 2022 Tori Kruse

ISBN: 978-1-66784-429-9

Dedication

I dedicate this book to the three people who have shaped my world. Mom, Dad, and Trav. You are the reason I believe in myself today and have chosen the path of perseverance. Thank you for always loving and supporting me through life's highs and lows. I will always be there for you. I love you with all my heart.

To every friend, coach, or mentor who has pushed me beyond my limits, helped deepen my faith in God, or strengthened the belief in myself, I'm forever grateful for you.

Jasmine Cochran, thank you for guiding me through this book-writing journey and helping me get my story out into the world. You have made this dream a reality and it wouldn't have been possible without you.

To the women reading this book: May you always realize your worth is not external but in everything internal that you are and who you're created to be. You are a beautiful gift to this world.

Table of Contents

Introduction

What's up, girl! You ready to have some fun? I know I am, and I'm so excited to take this ride with you!

The first thirty years of my life have been full of ups and downs, world travels, tears and laughter, losing myself and rebuilding myself again, and a million other moments I want to share with you. That's why I wrote this book.

I'm a small-town Iowa girl turned pageant queen turned entrepreneur. As I've made my way through all those titles, I've come to truly know and love who God created me to be through the process.

Every phase of my life has pushed me and shaped me in ways I never would have imagined. Growing up in Iowa, I knew anything was possible, but I knew none of the details. Through sports, my time as Miss Missouri USA, and the wild journey of making my mark as a businesswoman, I've had experiences that I just can't keep to myself. You're holding the lessons I learned through those experiences in your hand right now.

This book is a tool. If you read it with honest eyes and an open heart, you'll be equipped to use the strategies I've used to create the life you desire. Dive into the process, ask the hard questions, and follow my lead. The life you've always wanted is waiting on the other side!

In this book, you will see me completely unleashed. You'll see me celebrate myself, express my deepest hurts, be real about my failures, and work my plans for future wins. I'm proud of the journey I've walked for my first thirty years, including where I've been, who I've become, and where I'm going. Some parts have been rocky, some parts have been blissful, and other parts pure momentum. I don't sugarcoat or hide anything. This is my story in all its glory.

Get ready to stare your dreams in the face and go after them full throttle. Forget about what the world thinks of you and who it believes you should be. It's time to live your life the way you design it. It's go time. Live your life unexpected.

Enjoy the journey.

Chapter 1:

I BELIEVE IN YOU

Little did I know the lessons I learned in good ol' Glenwood, Iowa would stick with me forever. In a town with a population of six thousand, everybody knows everybody, which means everybody knows everybody's business. My parents owned a software company in town and would host their own seminars and conferences periodically. Dad ran the business and would sometimes travel a lot, but always kept family a top priority. My mom took care of the household, like the boss she is, and always made sure my older brother, Travis, and I were taken care of.

My mom was a rock star. Not only did she handle everything at home, but she was also the room mom at school and ran my brother and me all over town for our sporting events. Neither of my parents ever missed one of our many games. Dinnertime at our house was a sacred ritual, so much so that if Dad was ever late coming home, I'd bug him at work and call him every few minutes until he said he was on the way. I'm sure he loved me for that. My parents would always tell me how proud they were of me and that they believed in me. This core belief set a precedent for the rest of my life I'll never take for granted.

As entrepreneurs, my parents taught me most of the lessons that guide me today, not just professionally, but on a personal level as well. There were certain things they didn't tolerate, like quitting in the middle of an activity. If I didn't like a sport or organization, I had to finish the season—no questions asked. Whatever I chose to do, it was my responsibility to give it my all until the end. This family standard fueled my sense of perseverance. I had plenty of other characteristics consistent with entrepreneurial success, like an unquenchable drive to be the best at everything—basketball, jump rope, thumb war, arm wrestling—it didn't matter. When I think about it, I probably hated losing more than I loved winning. I believed I could do most things, but only if I could do them in my own unexpected way.

My entrepreneurial spirit bloomed at a young age. I remember walking into my dad's office when I was in elementary school to help prepare for my parents' upcoming conference. That's when I learned the importance of contribution and the gratification of being part of something greater than myself. I would bounce around the offices of my favorite employees and sit with them for hours, shooting the breeze, until my dad said, "Ok Tori, it's time to stop talking so my people can get back to work." I've always been drawn to people and their stories, and I was always excited to learn new things about the people who worked for my parents. I have a special curiosity about people who are much older than me or who have more experience than I do.

My parents cracked the business owner code. They could write their own book to tell you their fair share of failures. It took them many years to get to the point of freedom in their life, but they did it together and never gave up. It wasn't until about middle school when I realized something was different. Because of their success, my youth was spent traveling in our motorhome, spending weekends on our boat, and playing ball on our basketball court at home. We fished and camped on the weekends. When my brother and I were teenagers, our family of four would vacation for the month of July and travel a section of the States and up to Canada. I realized this wasn't common, so I felt even more grateful that our family had opportunities like this. These summer adventures led us to forty-eight states and nine Canadian provinces. Remember when I said I was from a small town where everybody knew everybody's business? Well, everybody knew about our motorhome excursions and our love for traveling, so when my brother and I would come back to school after being away all summer, we sometimes suffered the repercussions of bullies at school.

Some kids called us "moneybags" while others would stomp on my feet with their clunky shoes, making snarky comments under their breath. Girls commented on my makeup and "fancy jewelry," not knowing I'd gotten my earrings from Claire's and my makeup from the same convenience store they got theirs from. I tried to put on a tough kid front and act like it didn't bother me, but it actually stung every time someone would say something like this. I finally developed the nerve to joke back saying, "Me? Moneybags? I don't have a penny to my name. I'm broke as a joke," trying to make light of the situation to cover up my pain. This pattern quickly got old. No kid deserves to be bullied because of their upbringing, but thankfully our parents drilled the value of humility into us. With humility, you win in the long run.

That's not to say I always wanted to be humble; a chip on my shoulder might have given me the confidence I needed to tell the bullies to back off. Juggling airing my frustrations with humility and confidence was an internal conflict that took longer than my school years to master. I had to convince myself of my worth without letting my classmates see that I was trying to figure it out. To be clear, my parents' push for humility wasn't to hurt my confidence. It was because they believed in the motto, "Kill 'em with kindness." Looking back, I wish I would've had the moxie to speak my mind more.

Kids at school were doing what kids do, which made me all the more grateful for my brother. Trav and I have been best friends from the start. He's taught me more than I could ever give him credit for. Growing up, I hung around him and his friends because they were easy to relate to. Their humor, competitiveness, and lack of drama made them a safe and comfortable choice for whom to spend time with. I was just "one of the guys." Trav is the person who knows the most about me. He's my confidant, a straight shooter, and the person I respect the most. We've been through the best and worst times together, and because of that, we have each other's backs no matter what. It's not just the two of us. I have three sisters from my dad's first marriage, who all have children and families of their own. Growing up with a split family was a lot of fun when we all got together, although when I was younger, we definitely had our fair share of the ever-so-lovely "family meetings," but what family doesn't, right? It's funny how as a kid you don't understand all the dynamics, but as an adult it all kind of makes sense. Today, we're closer than we've ever been before.

My upbringing gave me a strong foundation for life, but everything wasn't always sunshine and rainbows. Losing loved ones at a young age had a strong impact on me. My brother and I were staying with my grandparents one night when we woke up the next morning to find that my sweet Grandma B had unexpectedly passed away at the age of sixty-six. I was eight years old. When I was a freshman in high school, my very daring and life-of-the-party eighteen-year-old cousin, Ryan, was in a fatal skateboarding accident. My junior year of high school, my best friend, who was actually dating my brother at the time, committed suicide. We were across the country, and I remember my friend Timothy calling to tell me the news, which I then had to break to my brother. Our family was in utter shock and despair. My dad drove the motorhome sixteen hours from Kentucky to Iowa to get home to the nightmare that awaited us. The devastation from this tragedy was compounded by seeing my brother in so much pain. All we could do in those devastating moments was lean on God, take it day by day, and share the beautiful memories we had of my dear friend Shari.

We are the sum of our experiences from the time we're born until now, but our childhood has the power to shape the thought patterns and behaviors we'll have as adults more than any other period in our lives. Harvard's Center on the Developing Child refers to this time of developing connections as "brain architecture," in which "our genes provide the blueprint, but experiences shape the process that determines if the brain will be a strong or weak foundation for future learning, behavior, and health." The signals in the brain that communicate to establish those factors quickly multiply and get stronger through repeated use. Guess what determines which ones are used the most? Our environment and experiences, or what people refer to as nature and nurture. People argue sometimes about which one has the bigger effect on how we turn out, but it's more a both/and situation than an either/or situation. The more an experience occurs, the more permanent the connections become. The connections that aren't used fade away. Through this process, our emotions, motor skills, behavior control, logic, language, and memory are solidified during the most critical period for growth in our lives. This is the foundation we build the rest of our lives on. Spending the first part of our lives in toxic environments weakens our brain architecture, which can interrupt our behavioral, physical, and mental health[1].

That's the scientific way to say that what happens to us during the most delicate time of our lives is what we carry with us throughout our lives. If your childhood wasn't the healthiest, you can reverse the damage by surrounding yourself with supportive people now[2] and establishing a growth mindset, a skill that will carry you through the rest of your life.

Your past has helped shape you. Whether that brings you comfort or scares you, it should excite you, because either way, you have the power to decide where your life goes now and every single day into your future! Who you become is up to you. Your childhood gives you clues to understanding why you are the way you are, but it's not there to keep you in a box. Anything that didn't work in your favor from before, turn it on its head. Make it a positive. Make it work for you. Don't be ashamed of who you are or where you're from. Those things are what made you who you are today.

I've had a darn good life. I've had a supportive, safe, loving, fun, and adventurous family and surroundings. Instead of feeling guilty for these blessings, I've learned to fully appreciate all that my parents worked so hard to give us. Even still, I've had to do a solid amount of internal work to unlearn limiting belief patterns and solidify empowering ones. Part of the human experience is creating the life we desire. I've had to experience loss so I could appreciate my wins, and I've had to learn how to reset my bravery and confidence each hour of each day when I was dealing with some of my darkest moments. We all have

---

1   https://developingchild.harvard.edu/science/key-concepts/
brain-architecture/

2   https://developingchild.harvard.edu/science/key-concepts/toxic-stress/

deep digging and heavy lifting to do to transform our mindset into one that sets us up for success, and it's not a one-time thing. A healthy mindset requires maintenance and care. If you feel like you have a long way to go, imagine how you'll feel when you put in the work and wake up one day having accomplished everything you wanted and more. Think about what it will feel like when someone comes up to you and says, "Because you went for it, you gave me the confidence to believe in myself, too." That's winning.

Chapter 2

PREPARE TO WIN

Any country music fans in the house? One of the best memories of my childhood was when my grandparents hosted exciting concerts at the fairgrounds they owned in Indiana that attracted country music lovers from all over the country. One summer when we went to visit my Grandma and Grandpa B at the fairgrounds, they had hired Faith Hill to come sing in concert. We were sitting in the front row, and I remember her pointing at me to come on stage. I was five years old and shy, so I didn't seize the moment, but dang if I could turn back time, I sure would now! Instead of trying to force me out of my comfort zone, she came down to where I was and sang a song. I didn't realize what she was doing then, but looking back, I admire her persistence to make others feel so special. She could have just ignored it and gone on with her concert, but instead, she chose to go out of her way to give me a memory I'll forever cherish.

In addition to Faith, I saw John Michael Montgomery, Brad Paisley, Leann Rimes, and Willy Nelson, to name a few. We got to meet them, tour their buses, and see them as normal people, not just celebrities on stage.

Those experiences are the reason I love country music so much today and why I appreciate great talent. Music tells a story, and the way those artists started small, persevered, and never gave up is exactly what I admire about them most. Those days were my introduction to realizing that anything is possible. We don't all have the same types of experiences growing up, but we all do have something valuable that drives us or trains our subconscious. What happened in your life that programmed your thinking today? Part of my programming was the value of old fashioned hard work.

There are no two ways around this: if you want to accomplish anything in life, you have to work for it.

The only way to success is through the process. If you think you can skip the work, your best bet is to buy a stack of lottery tickets, cross your fingers really hard, pray your sweet little heart out, and hope your numbers come up. Otherwise, you better get ready to weerrkkk sister. My parents modeled a strong work ethic for me as they built their business, but I learned it for myself by playing sports.

Basketball was my life from third grade to my senior year of high school. I played on a travel team and on my school's team. I was never the quickest, I could never jump the highest or rebound the best, but by God I'd try to outwork anyone who tried to beat me out, which earned me a spot on the starting five. I'd wake up at 6 a.m. to work on my free throws and three-point shot every day before school. Since my dad and brother would go to the gym with me and refuse to cut me any slack because I was a girl, I learned to be mentally tough and competitive.

Nothing got in the way of me working on my game. When we traveled, my mom scoped out campgrounds with a hoop so my brother and I could practice drills. Travel did NOT mean off-season. I've always had athletic ability, but it definitely didn't all come naturally; it took years of effort, day in, day out, to accomplish what I would ultimately accomplish in the game. In the end, working my butt off paid off. By the time I graduated from high school, I was the leading three-point shooter in my conference. The reason I was able to achieve this public recognition was because I'd put in the work when no one was watching. It made it easier to accept the times a couple of my teammates got a little cheeky because I'd taken vacation for a month, or that my coach talked about the risk of not starting me because I was missing summer practices. I practiced so dang hard behind closed doors that my results spoke louder than my words once the whistle blew.

I stayed ready, working hard so I could be on the varsity team all four years of high school. Determined to make a name for myself, my freshman and sophomore years, I suited up for one quarter of every varsity game. I'd be sitting at the end of the bench, just waiting for my coach to holler down in his hoarse, raspy voice, "Kruse! Get up here! We need you!" I can hear those words like they were said yesterday. I'd quickly toss off my warmup shirt and wait for Coach's instructions. He'd say, "Alright this is what we're going to do," then show me a play and tell me the team needed me to get open and make a three-point shot. With excitement and adrenaline running through my veins, I'd step in that varsity game as a freshman, ready to go head-to-head against a bunch of upperclassmen. Man, those were the moments I lived for. That's why you practice when no one is watching—for that three-second moment that can change the game. Work so that you're the person people believe in to take the shot when it counts the most.

Basketball wasn't my only love back then. When I was in seventh grade and Trav was in eighth, our school held a doubles ping-pong tournament. Determined to claim the title, we woke up every day at six (clearly it was my power hour at the time) to practice before we left for school. We worked on our serves. We worked on our backhand. We worked on our strategy and teamwork because we knew that's what was going to win us the championship. When the big day came around, Mom dropped Trav and me off at school full of anticipation, and we walked through the school doors dripping with confidence like the big bad middle-schoolers we were. It was game day. We had made it to the championship. PE class came around, and every one of our classmates gathered around us as we played the two best athletes in the school. Trav had been harassed the whole week leading up to this moment for partnering with his younger sister, but funny how the tough guys got quiet when we made the game-winning shot to take home the GOLD! Every time the score got close, Trav and I would encourage each other more. When one of us made a mistake, we would lift each other up instead of tearing each other down. When our mom picked us up from school that day, she screamed with excitement that we'd won. The next year, I worked just as hard and won the singles ping-pong championship of the school. I know ping-pong might not sound as thrilling as our favorite American pastimes, but believe me, it is! Plus, I take my sports seriously. No matter what the game is, I don't give up until I've given it my all. I realized at a young age what it takes to win, and my drive to succeed thankfully followed me from the court to the pageant stage.

When I was a freshman in college at the University of Iowa, I started my Miss USA journey by competing in Miss Iowa Teen USA. Even though I placed as a semifinalist, I wasn't crazy about pageantry at first and didn't immediately see it being a part of my life for the long term. After deciding I had unfinished business in the pageant world, I decided to go back a couple years later for Miss Iowa USA and, for the second time, placed as a semifinalist. I took two years from competition after that, graduated, moved to St. Louis, Missouri and tried again. The third time wasn't the charm. I was a semifinalist in Miss Missouri USA 2015. By then, I was committed to competing, but I had to take a step back and see what I needed to do to commit to winning. After all, if you're not first you're last, right?! I started finding coaches and mentors, but most foundationally, I found my purpose to win.

The next year, I placed second runner up. I wasn't discouraged; I was getting ready to go for it again the next year and win it all. The year after that, I placed first runner up. Ugh, that sucked. Have I said I hate losing yet? Every year I kept training more consistently until I made it my lifestyle. I made tremendous sacrifices for my dream. I worked on my mindset, studied the best, listened to my coaches and mentors, and fine-tuned my approach year after year. I spent countless hours visualizing the outgoing titleholder placing that crown on my head until my visualization became real. After my sixth time competing, everything finally fell into place. I was crowned Miss Missouri USA 2018, and I was on my way to compete in Miss USA 2018! A dream I had prayed about and tirelessly worked for had finally come to life.

Through this journey, I realized the road to success is paved with hearing a lot of "noes," accepting failures, welcoming obstacles, embracing sacrifice, and intentionally setting goals. The times my pageant journey stopped at semifinalist were opportunities for me to critique my performances and assess my plans. When you're spending so much of your life investing your time and energy into something you want to accomplish, you need to stop and ask yourself some critical questions. Are you documenting your process so you can figure out what to change and what to keep? Are you willing to take feedback from people who know more than you do without taking offense? Whatever you're trying to improve on, you can't do it if you don't know where you stand. You can't spend your energy comparing yourself to other people and becoming discouraged or being intimidated by somebody else's success. They're not your competition, anyway. You are.

When I was evaluating myself so I could switch things up to win the crown, I realized that I had to focus on winning the same way I'd focused on my three-point shot and ping-pong game back in school. I had to eliminate distractions and become singularly focused, even obsessed, on the goal. I had to show unwavering commitment to the process. When you're trying to be the best, you can't let distractions get in the way; it's mind over matter. You have to ask yourself everyday how bad you want it. When I reflected on how I'd prepared for those wins back then, I discovered some key takeaways:

1. Figure out why you want to win.

2. Don't just practice, but practice the right way.

3. Make it your lifestyle, not just a three-month quest.

4. Acknowledge every "no" as one step closer to your "yes."

5. Eliminate distractions.

6. Visualize exactly what you want on a daily basis.

7. Invest in mentors and coaches who have achieved what you want.

8. Develop the feelings of gratitude for the journey and feel them within your body.

9. Set achievable goals, write them down, and adjust them when necessary.

The difference between those who win and those who don't has more to do with consistency and dedication than it has to do with luck and talent.

You know how they say practice makes perfect? Well, that's not true if you're practicing the wrong technique. That's why coaches are so important. I figured that since I wasn't winning, there was a skill I hadn't nailed down yet, so I quit trying to figure it out for myself and decided to get insight by investing in people who had already achieved what I wanted for my future.

There aren't many resources more valuable than a coach. The same way a football or basketball coach can turn a losing team into a championship team in a year is the same way a pageant coach, business coach, or life coach can help you turn things around in your life. There are a lot of variables involved in pageantry. You may not be achieving your goals because of something small, and you might not even know what it is. Since 2010, I have hired over twenty-two coaches and mentors. Each of them has leveled up my life in a way I could've never imagined. Before my practice could make my performances "perfect," I needed to learn which skills and habits to improve and which ones to adjust.

Most of what we do is out of habit, especially when we're tired. That's why practice is called "conditioning." It's teaching your mind and body what movements and thoughts to rely on in each situation that might present itself in the heat of competition. If your practice is wrong, your performance will reflect that. But if your practice is right, your performance will be, too. In fact, studies suggest that "practice account[s] for about 80% of the difference between elite performance and amateur performance[3]."

Going from good to great requires three things from you: clarity, confidence, and consistency. Let's start with clarity.

CLARITY

A clear vision is crucial to a successful outcome. Creating a clear and concise plan of where you're going will help you recognize your small wins along the way. Start by setting audacious goals—bold, fearless goals—and write them down. This can't be something broad, like, "I want to be successful this year," or "I want to be better than I was last year." That's not a goal, that's a wish. Be specific about what you want, down to the details. If you leave room for confusion, you'll settle for mediocre results. This goal should make you uncomfortable—like unusually uncomfortable. It should be bigger than yourself. It should be something you're not equipped to do when you write it down because you haven't done the work yet. You should feel nervous about how far you have to go but excited at the thought of achieving something so tremendous.

Once you've written down that big goal, catch your breath, then write another goal or two that are a step further than the one you already wrote. Don't freak out at how big this goal seems when you see it on paper for the first time. Instead, embrace it. You know how to create magic where there is none. If you can see the dream behind your eyes, you can make it a reality in your life. If you're looking at those goals and they seem impossible, they won't seem that way after you break them down into pieces. What do you need to do monthly, weekly, even hourly to bring those big goals to fruition? The more specific you

---

3   https://www.verywellmind.com/
does-practice-really-make-perfect-2795158

get, the clearer your vision. Are you scared you're going to fail? Are you unsure if you'll be able to do in real life what you've thought up in your mind? Then it sounds like the next step is your cup of tea.

CONFIDENCE

I'm not joking or exaggerating when I say I've hired over twenty-two coaches to continually improve my confidence and performance. I want to get all the insight I can from experts who've paved the way so I can become the best I can be. And let me tell you, there's nothing more gratifying than putting in the work and watching your wildest dreams become reality. Take a minute to let your imagination run wild. Imagine yourself reaching your pinnacle. You've done it. You put in the effort, you're living your dream. What do you feel? What's going through your mind? What sounds do you hear? What's happening in your stomach, your heart? How big is the smile on your face? Stop right now and write all of those answers down. When you write down all of your feelings on paper, they start to become real.

So now that you've written down all the feelings you'll feel once you're victorious, ask yourself, "Is this goal the ultimate goal, or is it a stepping stone? Will it move me toward something else later?" What benefits are going to follow?" Then start to create a practice schedule for your dream. The more you practice, the more confidence you'll have. The only reason I truly feel confident in anything I do is because I over-prepare for "game time." Some people think there's a crazy method to confidence, but I can tell you quickly how to gain confidence by doing two things: creating a plan and practicing your butt off. No excuses.

CONSISTENCY

Ohhh this ever-so-lovely word. Consistency. Whew. It's not always easy, is it? But if I'm being real, if a dream matters to you, you have no choice but to stay consistent if you want to achieve it. In order to get ahead, you have to be disciplined and show up when you don't feel like it. Do that extra lift at the gym, make that next sales call, go to Bible study, read that chapter before you go to bed. Keep your goals at the forefront so you can stay motivated on the days that you just want to sit on your couch and eat popcorn in front of the television. You are the total of your everyday decisions. If you spend your time doing things that don't matter, those habits will expose you.

What do you do each day to move yourself closer to your goal? Are you reading books to help develop a winning mindset? Do you journal? Count your blessings or complain about your frustrations? Meditate? Spend so much time watching television that you can give a rundown of every binge-worthy series on every viewing platform? Be careful about the external stimuli you're letting in. Don't watch too much negative news, and don't spend too much time on social media scrolling through the mumbo jumbo that isn't inching you closer to your future self. Be selfish with the minutes that you have in a day and make sure they are always helping you move from point A to point B, both personally and professionally.

If you feel more stressed than excited right now at the thought of achieving your goals, think about why that is. If you're questioning whether the goals you wrote down will ever make it off the page, maybe you are struggling with limiting beliefs, or a thought pattern that restricts you in some way. Don't believe every thought that crosses your mind. Oftentimes our mind tries to talk us out of everything we're called to become. Once you recognize you have a belief that is limiting you, focus on reframing that belief so it serves you and your bigger vision. For example, if you want to increase your social media following for your business but you're thinking, "I don't know how to increase my following. Nobody likes what I post," you can flip that belief and say, "My social media is growing rapidly because I am showing up as my authentic self every day." Your mindset determines everything for you, but YOU have to create that mindset! You can't just wish or write something and have it magically manifest for you; you have to balance desire with action and show the universe you're willing to work at something. Hold yourself accountable to your dreams. If you don't, they'll die with you.

You have to push when you don't feel like it, when it's inconvenient, and when it means you have to sacrifice something. Time is not going to wait for you, so you have to use the minutes to perfect your craft. The year 2020 handed us a global pandemic. That was a difficult time that brought up a lot of unknown feelings, but I can tell you one thing: Challenging times expose the people who have been doing the internal work and those who haven't. When times get tough, do you press in or back down? When times get crazy around you, it's important to have something consistent, a practice that can anchor you. Hopefully that anchor is your belief in yourself and the practices that back that up. If you practice consistently, when it comes game time, you don't have to think twice about confidence; it will come naturally. When you do everything in your power to succeed, nothing will tear you down.

Chapter 3

THE POWER OF EXPOSURE

Back in 2012 when I was a junior in college, I studied international marketing for six weeks in Florence, Italy. While I was there, I found an internship in a boutique where I had to research and tag clothing. In Italian. Which I didn't speak. I failed miserably, to say the least. Laugh it up.

Fortunately, I didn't explore Italy alone. My brother, a senior at the University of Iowa at the time, studied overseas with me. Like the opening scene of a classic horror story, a big white van met us and a bunch of other college students at the airport to take us to our homes for the next six weeks. We pulled into an alleyway full of graffiti, which I would later learn was a respected form of art in Italian culture, when the driver called my name along with two other girls'— one from Alabama, the other from Colorado. I didn't know what we were doing in that alley, but I had my brother there to help me fight in case something was about to go down. It didn't; the driver was just dropping us off there because, as unsettling as it seemed at the time, that's where our apartment was. I waited for my brother to get out the van, but he never did. He would be living somewhere else, which neither of us knew until that moment. We had no cell phone service, so I didn't know how to get in touch with him or even when I would see him again.

"See you soon, I guess?" I said to Trav before the driver handed me my key and the van pulled off.

There I was, in an Italian alleyway with two girls I didn't know, mounds of luggage, the key to my new home, and no idea where my brother was going. Did I mention it was pouring down rain?

The other two girls and I looked at each other, introduced ourselves, and figured, "Well, guess we're roommates for the next six weeks. Let's do this!" On the outside, I was cool and collected, but under the surface, I was beyond scared about how any of this was going to work out. What else could I do but gather my stuff along with my composure and face the unknown?

We turned the brown iron handles on the gigantic wooden door and stepped into the pitch-black lobby of our apartment building. My two new friends and I slowly peeked around the corner like a fluffle of scared bunnies. The walls were wooden, the floor was cobblestone, and the lobby was desolate. Right around the corner was a staircase that led to our apartment door. We found a tiny light in the staircase. Score! We clicked it on, lugged our huge suitcases up the stairs, and made our way inside. I'd never seen a kitchen so small. We looked around and saw a washer, but no dryer, so we would have to hang our clothes to dry—FOR SIX WEEKS. I picked a room with twin beds and pushed them together to make a larger bed. It still felt nothing like home. The toilet in the bathroom had a bidet, which I had never in my life seen or used before. But I guess there is a time and place for everything, even if that means cleaning your booty from the toilet seat! This place was shaping up to be nothing like I'd imagined.

We explored our new home for a while until it was time to meet at registration later in the afternoon. I learned real quick that the way Italians gave directions was nothing like I was used to. When the driver originally dropped us in the alley, he'd said, "Ok, registration for your program is between three and six near the McDonald's, it's down the alley, to the right, then go through the Piazza de la (whatevertheheck-they'recalled), then take your second left around the corner, and then make another two rights and it'll be on your left."

Yeah, thanks for the clarity. We'll be on time for sure.

He gave us a paper map that had gotten damp from the rain. We figured we could find the directions online, but our phones only worked for two seconds here and there because of our apartment's spotty Wi-Fi. At this point, I was more than nervous about this whole arrangement; I added lost and confused to the hodgepodge of emotions inside of me. I wish I could tell you things got better the next day. They didn't.

The next night, feeling comfortable enough to explore our new city, my roommates and I went out for dinner and drinks. Late in the evening, we walked back up our dark alleyway and turned the corner to discover two men who had been following us home. They whispered back-and-forth to each other, and the closer we got, the more suspicious they seemed. Thanks to my mom, I've always been aware of my surroundings; I knew what to do.

"We're in trouble if we open our lobby door," I said to the girls, "so just act calm and keep walking like we don't live here so they don't know which door is ours." As we walked on, they walked by us and stopped, hollered at us, and tried to stop us. When we sped up more, they turned around to follow us. I could feel my heart pounding in my chest. I didn't know where to find help, and of course, the streets were empty. I told the girls we needed to run and find the nearest hotel; somebody would be there who could help us.

We turned the corner and sprinted down the street, but there was no hotel in sight, so we stopped in a convenience store where I bought a huge can of bug spray to use for mace. We left the store, went back around the corner, and peeked back down the alleyway, bug spray locked and loaded. Bold and persistent, the two men were standing right in front of our door, waiting for us to come back. We turned back around and eventually found a hotel where we could call the "polizia." They arrived and asked what was going on. After we gave them the rundown, they escorted us to our apartment and up to our room. The two men weren't there, but I couldn't help but wonder if they were lurking around, trying to find a way in.

I was shook. I just knew those guys would come back. They knew where we lived and seemed determined to get to us, and we still had five weeks, five days, six hours, and forty-two minutes in that apartment building. I spent many sleepless nights wondering if they were lingering outside our door. But you know what? They never showed up again, and the rest of my time in Italy was adventurous and enlightening, the bliss I imagined it would be when I was prepping to get on the plane to see what life was like on the other side of the world.

That night running from those guys taught me you can never be too aware, especially as a woman. I had the time of my life living in Italy and exploring Europe. Meeting new friends from all over the world was priceless. I learned important lessons, like always be aware of your surroundings, don't go a day without espresso and a pastry in Italy, drink the vino in Tuscany, oh, and pay attention in class.

I'm the type of girl who likes to be ready for the camera. Yep, I said it. I might as well own up to it. So that means I like to be halfway presentable when I step outside of my door in the morning, hair and makeup ready. Because of that, plus being tall and blonde, you can imagine that I stuck out like a sore thumb in Italy. Every day as I would walk past the market, I was asked by a local guy if I was from California. I mean, come on—it doesn't get more stereotypical than that! In Italy, they go for the natural look, so with my hairstyles, makeup, and per- fumes, I may as well have had a flashing sign above my head that said "TOURIST." It only took a week of feeling uncomfortable before I decided to kick the high maintenance version of Tori to the curb and embrace their natural culture. I dressed more simply, I let my hair go, and my full face of makeup was scaled down to a little bit of mascara. The change felt strange but freeing at the same time. I didn't need to impress anyone. Day by day, I became more comfortable in my own skin. I was also single and convinced I was going to find my husband there, but after that second-day scare, I think the only man I spoke to was whoever was serving me wine, espresso, or pastries.

My new look wasn't the only simple thing about my stay. When I got there, they gave me a Nokia cell phone that only had calling and a few texting capabilities. There was no Wi-Fi, no apps, no notes, no nothing—just numbers and a call button. It was quite the adjustment from my smartphone with its built-in friendly robot assistant.

After I'd adapted to the natural look and grown fond of the graffiti, Italy ended up stealing my heart. However! The simple holes in the ground used for public toilets tested my aim and leg strength. Everything looked beautifully dated in this historic land where the idea of cleanliness is much different from our American germaphobeness.

Their public transit was convenient, and you could even drink wine on the trains, so you know they sure as heck had me sold! Italians understand that it's the moments that come together to make up your life, so they appreciate them in a way Americans spend good money to figure out. Nobody there was in a rush. Life in Italy was simple. I appreciated my calm there, but at the same time, it made me appreciate home even more.

Italy's five-star hotels were like our three-star hotels. Our technology is more advanced, our food scene is more varied, and there are endless resources and opportunities. But then again, all these things make me miss the way they do things in Europe. People worked through the night to make sure the local bakeries were stocked with fresh pastries in the morning all around the city. People smiled and said, "Ciao bella!" as they walked through the market, and we walked pretty much everywhere we went (which is probably why I only gained five pounds there, even though a pastry and espresso were part of my everyday morning routine). Their way was an inspiration to me and taught me about gratitude, appreciation, being in the moment, and joy. I didn't feel like I needed to be on a constant grind to make the next dollar or have the best car. I could just be grateful for what I had and the unlimited opportunities around me.

As you can probably tell, the experience of being in Italy left a bigger impression on me than the studies that took me there in the first place. My international marketing teacher had taught in six different countries and knew the languages from all of them. The class was ridiculously tough, and I didn't study but a smidgen (sorry, Mom and Dad). On test days, I'd cram in the library two hours before test time with friends, pastries, and espressos. I always made Cs, while my friends would ace the assessments (I've never been accused of being the best test-taker). While I don't advocate blowing off your tests or assignments, I am saying whatever you're doing and wherever you are, be sure to soak in every part of the experience. I certainly made that a priority. Since our class only met twice a week, we had time to explore a new city almost every weekend.

The Amalfi Coast was my favorite. On the way there, my friends and I grabbed a cheap Marilyn Monroe cooler from the local convenience store, along with a couple of bottles of our favorite beverages, and rented a small boat to take out on the Mediterranean Sea. We laughed, cried, jumped in crystal waters, and soaked up the sun. Moments with friends and family are sacred, especially in places you know you won't be forever.

Those six weeks in Italy lit a fire in me to explore other cultures and embrace what the locals do. It takes being where they are and dipping your toes into their everyday experiences to be able to see life through perspectives outside your own. They say studying abroad will either be your best decision or your worst mistake. Amen to that. Travel is my portal into new worlds. Italy was an exposure trip that pushed me into higher levels of thinking, seeing, and expanding. Fortunately, foreign travel isn't the only way to capture those experiences. Adventure is all around if you have the eyes to see it. Where in your city have you not been? Who do you see on the regular but haven't spent time with or gotten to know? What are you resisting being exposed to? Italy taught me there's more to life than my comfort zone and gave me a microscope to explore reality in ways I hadn't considered before.

When you think about the person you ultimately want to become and line it up against the person you are now, how are you the same and how are you different? Going through our everyday routines has a way of insulating us from what's happening in the rest of the world. It also has a way of convincing us that the way we do things is the best or even the only way, but when you step out of your comfort zone, you realize there are many ways to reach the same end. You learn about your own open-mindedness and flexibility. Your varied experiences give you something to compare to so you can decide if you're living at your highest possible level. With the right mindset, you can do that anywhere.

Near or far, adventure is everywhere. Looking within and developing your self-awareness are the greatest adventures you'll ever have, and what you learn on that journey will stay with you forever. Let's walk that path together and take the necessary steps from who you are to who you want to be.

Chapter 4

JUGGLING A HUMBLE CONFIDENCE

The single most determining factor in your success or failure is the belief you have in yourself. It's not so much about the material things you do or don't have. While your environment and upbringing play a role, your success mostly depends on whether or not you believe you can do it and the actions you take to follow up with that belief.

No matter what has happened to us in the past, we have the ability to rewire our brains at any age. Depending on their past life experiences and upbringing, this may be more difficult for some. Facing your past and making changes comes with a great deal of awareness, growing pains, and learning moments. Despite what you've believed about yourself in the past, how cool is it that you always have the option to change your thinking and build the confidence you desire? But the choice is up to you. By replacing negative beliefs with a positive thought pattern and getting out of your comfort zone, you'll grow the confidence you already have and build the capacity to expand it.

Our society has changed drastically in the past few years, especially when it comes to gender roles and socially acceptable behavior for women. Now, I'm not saying we don't still have a hill to climb, but at least we're making substantial headway. We can thank the female warriors who came before us for that! We have to continue to live full out, take ownership of the results we bring into our lives, and break any limiting beliefs we have stemming from the past. We all have a choice. My prayer is that we all continue to rise up and step into our full power! Recognizing your talents and power, but being careful not to be boastful or arrogant, is a tricky balance. That's what I call a humble confidence.

Confidence and cockiness can easily be confused or misinterpreted, but one thing I've realized is when you treat others how you want to be treated, you can't lose. On the other hand, when you downplay your success, talent, beauty, or wherever else, you shine in the name of humility, but you know you're the bee's knees, so you're being fake. Plain and simple. The problem is an either/or lens through which people see these traits. I want to make it clear that you can have both. Confidence and humility are not mutually exclusive. But they can be a hard balance, am I right?!

Humility is a beautiful trait because it keeps you grounded, makes you likable, and reminds you that you have room to grow. Most individuals gravitate toward humble people. All the word means is "to have a modest opinion of your own importance." It might sound kind of boring, but it's an amazing concept if you think about it like this: You are not less or more important than anybody else. Not only are you capable of offering your unique gifts, talents, and skills to the world, but so are the people around you. If you love yourself, celebrate yourself. And if you love others, celebrate them, too. There is enough love, recognition, and champagne to go around. Seek to understand others and acknowledge their value in this world, and they'll never have a problem with your confidence. Being humble means you are not proud or arrogant. It doesn't mean you're not supposed to love yourself or recognize what you do well. Arrogance is often an expression of a lack of confidence. To be arrogant means you think you're superior or entitled, and you need people to know it. How does confidence correlate with that? It doesn't. That's why we're calling BS on the whole idea.

Some people can be threatened by confidence because they don't think there's enough to go around, or maybe they see something in you they wish they had. Instead of dimming your light to protect their egos, maybe you can be a leading example of how to be a boss without a chip on your shoulder.

When you feel good about yourself, but you don't feel confident around other people, things start to get interesting. False humility leads to putting yourself down (which there's never a need for) or playing dumb, pretending like you don't know you're awesome. I've seen people in the middle of doing what they're best at, right in the flow of the expression of their dreams, minimizing every ounce of work they've done because they don't want people to think they think too highly of themselves. You've seen this too, and you've probably done it. I know I have. But no more, suckaaaaa!

I'll never forget this one client that I had, a college student I was coaching on mindset and confidence. She was in a heavily male-dominated film class, which was totally not a problem with her. Until it was. She would find herself majorly lacking confidence without knowing why. She told me she always poked fun at herself and her work. Keep in mind, this girl was smart. Brilliant. We couldn't let her keep dimming her light. Once she told me she'd been making herself small to fit in with her class, I coached her through the process of understanding why she was lacking confidence. We figured out the reason she made jokes about her work was because she had a fear of failure, so joking about her skills was a protective mechanism in case she got crappy feedback. She was using self-deprecating humor the entire time, which served no one—especially not herself.

Listen to me: it is not your job to make other people feel comfortable, especially when you have to make less of yourself to do it. How other people respond to your success is their responsibility. Don't allow someone to steal your flame and your talents. You have a world to bless and a soul to satisfy.

Confidence is precious because it takes so much work to get and even more work to maintain. When you finally figure out how to do something difficult, or win that thing you've been fighting for, or convince yourself to try something you thought you could never do, confidence blossoms. Once you have it, you're not willing to let it go or substitute it for cheap replacements. Even when you're knocked down, if somebody tries to steal your confidence, you can bet they ain't getting it without a fight.

When I first started competing in pageants, I thought I had to have everything perfectly in place. I had to look a certain way, walk a certain way, wear a certain gown, and have my hair, makeup, and spray tan perfect before I could win. I did all those things and kept getting right to the edge of winning, but I couldn't get over the hump. The move that made the biggest difference was changing my mindset and building my confidence. It was the inner work that yielded the results I'd been working so hard for.

I grew up in a household where humility was paramount. We focused on talking about our wins, but we always also critiqued them, focusing on how we could have done better. We realized we had been blessed with our circumstances, and we were compassionate toward those who were not as fortunate. We knew to always treat everyone equally. I'm so grateful for that mindset, but growing up in it, I also struggled with balancing humility and confidence. I think it was hard for me mainly because I didn't realize there was a difference between confidence and arrogance. The only way I knew how far was too far when talking about success was when my dad would say, "Oookay Tori, let's not get too carried away now." Then I'd chuckle and keep telling my story, not to brag, but to share my excitement with the people I loved. The more of those stories I had, the more my confidence grew.

Would you believe me if I told you one of the years I won the swimsuit award at Miss Missouri, I didn't even perform my best? During the swimsuit portion of the competition, I walked off the stage the completely wrong way. Yes you read that correctly; I walked off stage the completely wrong way and I still won. I couldn't believe it! In the middle of my walking pattern, I went the opposite direction off stage and thought to myself, CRAP—I just messed up the walking pattern! Simultaneously, I thought to myself, Keep going, you got this! Just act like it didn't happen, stand tall, smile and do your thing, act like it was planned. I stood proud and walked my walk. Wrong direction. Wrong exit. But I owned it. Confidence doesn't mean you don't make mistakes. It does mean you're comfortable enough with yourself to understand a mistake can't break you, and if it does, you can get back up and rebuild.

Losing can be a big punch in the gut to your confidence. I lost five state pageants before I finally won. Five! That's more than five years of training that didn't give me the results I worked for. It would have been easy to give up, decide pageantry wasn't for me, convince myself I couldn't do it, and throw my six-inch heels in the back of the closet. In fact, when I was on the bus with a bunch of other contestants transporting to the auditorium during my first pageant, some of the contestants were saying they'd competed six times. I sat there and thought to myself, Giiiiive it up, already! Obviously I didn't say that out loud, but my thinking was if it hadn't happened yet, it probably wasn't going to. Then look at what happened. Six years later, that was me. Karma will make you bite your tongue, won't it? After that, I got it. It was their belief that kept them going, and they weren't stopping until they got what they came there for. Each time I returned to the stage, my confidence increased. Not naturally, but because I spent hours every day working toward that winning moment. Each time, I was closer to my yes.

Dusting yourself off, getting back up, and trying again is an act of bravery. After losing so many times, I could have been embarrassed and gone down another path, but I didn't view my losses as failures. I took those losses as learning opportunities to say, "Ok, I grew a bit through this, and I need to be honest about other areas where I can grow as well." All the coaches and mentors I've worked with over time had a hand in building me up. I was riding off their belief in me before I believed in it myself. Because our energies were working towardl the same goal, I could trust them to push me further.

When you compete again and again at something, getting back up boils down to perseverance. Whatever you want is worth having, even if you can't have it right now. Pageantry isn't a team sport, and because it's so individual, everything falls back on you. You have to take ownership and responsibility for your results. Only you can do the work. You can't hide or blame anybody else, so you have to put in time and effort behind closed doors so you're proud of the results everyone will see when you're under the stage's spotlight. I was able to wake up each day and do that work because of my faith, my family, and my coaches. Because of them, not only did my confidence stay intact, but my skills grew as well.

A common piece of advice that people give about confidence is, "Fake it 'til you make it." That's a scary saying. If you learn to operate through fakeness from the beginning, you build habits on artificial values. Those are habits you don't want, if you ask me! You won't just wake up one day and flip a switch to realness. As you improve and become more successful, you'll have to keep being fake because it's the foundation you've built everything on. Eventually, the cracks in the foundation will catch up to you. You'll crack easily under pressure. No façade lasts forever, so there's nothing better than being yourself from the start!

It's possible to do things before you have the confidence to do them, kind of like the time I walked across hot coals at the Tony Robbins conference that were a thousand degrees Fahrenheit. That's where I upgraded my title to "Firewalker." Confidence isn't a precursor to action. So often, you have to act while you're scared or feeling unprepared and learn the lessons on the way. The way to achieve ultimate confidence is proving to yourself you can do what needs to be done despite the circumstances. Saying it is easier than doing it, but You. Can. Do. It.

These lessons are especially hard for perfectionists. Yep, that's me. And if that's you too, highlight this line: don't compare your Chapter Three to someone else's Chapter Ten. Do your best with everything you have. If you don't feel good about doing something or putting your work into the world until it's without flaw, take a deep breath and remember how far you've come. We don't live in a perfect world, and you aren't going to change that. Doing something now, taking those steps toward success, is better and smarter than wasting time waiting on perfection. Be so focused on who you're becoming through the process that you keep your blinders on to the external world and what is expected of you. When I go back and look at my old coaching videos online, I shake my head, laugh, and smile. A little bit of it is out of embarrassment, but more of it is out of the fact that I'm so dang proud that I had the courage to step outside of my comfort zone even when I was farrrr, I mean FAR from the best. Those videos helped me get where I am today. They're like watching game film and critiquing my performance from my basketball days. Although I didn't promote them too much on social media back then, those videos were proof to myself that I could set my mind to a goal and achieve it, no matter what. What is that one thing you have been procrastinating on because your confidence is lacking? Go do it within the next seven days. Don't try to make it perfect. Just do it. Prove to yourself that you can follow through with a goal that's been lying dormant in your heart. Moving forward through your fears isn't faking anything at all. It's what warriors do.

While I was Miss Missouri USA, I was in a relationship that completely shook my confidence. I had to fight through feelings of doubt and uncertainty every single day. My energy and confidence were drained, and I felt more insecure than I had in a long time. Many confident people go through similar things, even if they never share them. My morning routine and time with God kept my mindset on track and helped me focus on the end goal. Fighting my way through that time in my life just further confirmed that I can do things that seem impossible and come out better on the other side. I didn't do it alone though, and you don't have to either.

I follow certain practices to keep my confidence in place. I'm a proponent of therapy and counseling. At any given time, the world is overwhelming, and while the world is going crazy, you're dealing with your own personal struggles, too. If you need to seek professional help, you have not failed. In addition to seeing a therapist, I have a daily practice of reading scriptures and journaling my thoughts. Journaling gets all the stories, stressors, and fears out of your head and onto paper where you can see them more clearly. Additionally, I write down a list of things I'm grateful for every day and visualize my dreams, and I'm always investing in my personal growth. I'm never without a coach or mentor who's pushing me to be more. I encourage my clients to have coaches, so I focus on leading by example, not by my words. My goal is to be authentic and create a space where others have the freedom to do the same. I also have to remind myself that no matter what I do, no matter how many action steps I take, things won't fall into place until it's time.

Because of my faith, I believe in God's timing for the milestones in my life, so when something doesn't go my way, instead of stewing in bitterness, frustration, and resentment, I lean in further to His word. It challenges me to keep life in perspective. You can do everything right and still get first runner up. I'm not talking about just pageants, I'm talking about anything in life. So you're not winning right now. Okay. Consider this your continued education, because I can guarantee you there's a lesson in the journey. I want to remind you that your worth is not based on first place. It's based on who you are to Him and how true you are to yourself.

They say comparison is the thief of joy. I would go as far as saying it can also rob our self-confidence. It's especially easy now to compare yourself to other people because their highlight reels are available to us 24/7. Since social media has taken over our lives, it's easy to look at the accounts you're following and assume those people are all the way put together and have cracked the code to life. Can I just be the first to tell ya—they haven't! People online can make their lives look like movie trailers, and without taking a second to think, we immediately believe what we're seeing on the screen. Sometimes we get into the trap of comparison and jealousy, two things that will never help you find the success you're looking for. I'm a big fan of seeing people's positivity but with the understanding and awareness that they also have their difficult moments and struggles. No one's life is perfect. I personally find joy in sharing my ups and downs because I figure if sharing my struggle helps just one person, then it was worth the post. Vulnerability is just as valuable (if not more) as showing the amazing parts of my life that I'm grateful for. My struggles are what make me real and human. Transparency is one of my core values, and I welcome you to jump on that train too.

It took me a while to get here though. When I was competing, I was polishing myself up to be what people expected me to be; that was the name of the game, right? My years of competition were transformative years, heavily influenced by pageantry. I was convinced I had to act, walk, talk, and be a certain way. Then I realized, when I finally won, that even in pageants, winning wasn't about the external. It was in the internal work where I peeled back the layers of who I was and became the real me. Failure teaches you authenticity because you learn more about yourself when you lose than when you win.

Although I've worked extensively on my own self-confidence, I'm not exempt from moments of lapse. One day, I caught myself comparing myself to a woman who popped up on one of my social feeds. I didn't know who she was or why her picture affected me the way it did, but I took a moment and paid attention to what I was feeling. When you compare, check yourself and identify what's lacking in you instead of ignoring it and letting those emotions fester. If you're comparing yourself to someone you admire for motivation because they inspire you, engage in that. This is healthy. But if comparisons leave you feeling inferior or superior, it's time to do some inner work. Either way, when you have moments that cause you to question yourself, appreciate them. They're showing you where you still need to improve.

No matter how it looks from where you sit, everybody on this planet is dealing with something. Even people who are considered experts in their field have doubts, fears, and overwhelming moments. Experts get to expert status because they do the deep internal work day in, day out to heal the broken sides of themselves. When your confidence begins to unravel, go back to the old faithful and use your winning routines to build it back up. Your future self will thank you.

Chapter 5

DOES THIS MAKE MY BUTT LOOK BIG?

Let's be real. If you talked to somebody else the way you talk to yourself sometimes, you would have to know Brazilian Jiu-Jitsu to keep them off of you. They wouldn't tolerate it! But for whatever reason, we think it's okay to harp on our every flaw and tell ourselves stories about the way we look and our personalities, or point out our every mistake. Then, we can't figure out why we feel so down all the time! It doesn't make any sense to be careful with what you say to others but unforgiving in the way you talk to yourself. What have you said to yourself so far today? Think about the conversations—just today—that've happened in your head, or even out loud. How much of it has been negative and how much of it has been positive? Don't lie to yourself.

For so many years now, I've seen women self-sabotaging through sarcasm and even over-humility, or simply by not even accepting a compliment. We've all been there before, right? "Oh my gosh Tori your hair looks so cute like that!" "Omigosh, no get out of here I just threw it up in a messy bun." Come on girl, you're better than that. Just smile and accept the love. Don't degrade your beauty when someone compliments you. The perfect response is a humble thank-you. Confidence can be genuine, it can be developed, and it can be yours.

What you think about yourself is the single most important factor in the success you will or won't have. Self-perception has the power to drown you in anxiety and depression. It also has the power to build you up like a fortress and carry you through times when difficult circumstances are trying to destroy you. We truly have that much power in our heads. Our thoughts become our words, and our words become our reality, so before we can correct what we say to ourselves, we need to adjust our thinking.

Olympians work as hard as they do because they have the core belief that they can win the gold. People attempt climbing Mt. Everest because they believe they can make it to the top. Entrepreneurs start businesses because they believe they can provide a product or service to the public in a way no one else can. However, if your belief isn't strong, staying consistent long enough to win is going to be tough. You'll go through life accepting "good enough" and never pushing to discover your fullest potential. Those who believe they can accomplish whatever they put their minds to and find solutions to challenges operate from empowering beliefs. Those who find a problem for every solution and hold themselves back due to fear or artificial "realism" operate from limiting beliefs.

Our self-worth is heavily determined by our past. A mixture of the viewpoints you picked up from your parents, friends, and teachers, your accomplishments and failures, and a variety of other factors help shape this. Your self-esteem can also be altered by advertisements, social media, movies, and magazines. Fortunately, recent diversity efforts have spotlighted the reality that beauty is multifaceted. It spans age, ethnicity, and size. Before, if you didn't fit the mold, it's easy to understand why your self-worth would suffer. Today, as the world becomes more and more open to the expanding boundaries of beauty, intelligence, talent, and creativity, people are feeling more seen than ever. I'm for anything that can help convince you of your greatness. If you don't sprinkle it throughout the world while you're here, the rest of us will miss out on what you came here to offer. You are more than what people see on the surface. Please do yourself and the rest of the world a favor and never lose sight of how valuable you are.

When I was training for Miss Missouri USA in 2015, I decided to go all in. I was done losing and was ready to do everything it took to finish pageant night with the crown on my head. Part of the game plan was my diet. By the time I hired my trainer, I was confident in my knowledge of nutrition, but it turned out I'd been eating wrong for years. I wasn't eating enough, and when I was eating, I was choosing the wrong foods at the wrong time of day. During the consultation with my trainer, I knew my education about health was about to grow exponentially. Knowing where it would lead, just for good measure, I asked him a question I already knew the answer to.

"Can I still drink on this program?"

"Well, what do you drink?" he asked.

"Coffee, water, and around six thirty I'll occasionally pour myself a nice little glass of full body cabernet," I smiled, "and if I go out on the weekend for dinner, I might just have myself a nice, crisp dirty martini . . . with some olives . . . stuffed with blue cheese." He was laughing by now.

"I guess it all depends on how bad you want to reach your goals."

I wanted those goals more than a sweet tooth craving donuts. So that was it. Bye-bye fun cocktails; I'll see you after the pageant.

The more I learned about nutrition, the more obsessed I became. I took the supplements he recommended even though my momma fiercely opposed them. But that didn't last long; my body didn't react to them well, and we were looking for what would work. I followed my nutritionist's plan like it was the roadmap to the promised land. I ate enough chicken and broccoli to feed a tour bus of bodybuilders, and I would even ask servers at restaurants how many ounces of meat were in their servings because I didn't want to go over my allowed portion. The plan was the plan! Thankfully, part of that plan was the freedom to indulge in one cheat meal per week. I lived for those meals. I planned cheat meals for the next week as soon as I finished the one I was eating. I only got one a week. I couldn't waste it.

Although I was getting super fit, the world of fitness and nutrition was swallowing me up. If I missed one workout or ate something that wasn't on my list, I would be on edge, anxious that I was going to ruin my chances of winning. I became overly cautious of messing up. What was meant to elevate me was slowly becoming dangerous for my mental health. When I look back on this time of obsessive nutrition, a series of three events should have alerted me to pump the brakes.

One morning, I went to my kitchen to start my coffee maker. I sat on my couch to read the Scriptures before heading to the gym at my new power hour, 5:30 a.m. I got dressed, grabbed my bag, and was ready to start the day. And then I looked down. It was only three . . . IN THE MORNING.

I was wound up so tightly, so scared to do something wrong, that I was waking up spontaneously, full of adrenaline, entirely too early. I wasn't getting enough rest, and my anxiety was ramping up. That morning, the sirens began going off in my head. I was losing control to this nutrition obsession.

A different day, as I was pumping gas into my car, I turned around to walk to the driver's side door and randomly broke down into tears. At that moment, I wanted nothing more than to go inside the gas station and buy some chips, sour candy, an energy drink or anything that would make my taste buds dance, but I told myself, "No, that's not going to serve your goals." I was so sick of telling myself no all the time.

Hanging out with friends for happy hour? No.

Going out to dinner at a fun restaurant? Girl, do you know how much sodium they put in their food? No.

Adding seasoning to my own food? How is that seasoning going to serve you? Sacrifice today so you can win tomorrow. No.

Skipping one—just one—session of forty-five-minute cardio because I was exhausted? Nah.

And this day, gas station candy. Something that had seemed so inconsequential before now felt like it had complete control over me. Making no allowances except that one weekly cheat meal was over-whelming physically and mentally, but I knew if I wanted to compete and win, I needed to be in the best shape of my life. I didn't realize I also needed to be in the best mental and emotional shape possible, and what I was doing to myself physically was destroying that.

Until that moment at the gas station when I was mourning candy on the shelf, I hadn't realized my mental state was suffering. While I never considered harming myself, I realized I was on the verge of depression, and something needed to change.

I said heck with it. I got in my car and drove straight to the best burger drive-in in St. Louis, a tiny little spot that only takes cash. That place has to be what heaven smells like. Feeling like a rebel, I darted toward the bar, sat on a stool, and ordered a double cheeseburger with fries and a root beer, all words I hadn't uttered in what seemed like years. I felt like I had broken some chains. Did I care that I was going to be on stage in a bikini in less than a month? Not at all. This was soul food. Without this burger smothered in cheese from the holy dairy farms of America, the crisp edges of those perfectly salted fries, and the bubbles of the root beer popping the sides of my cheeks, I might have been miserable for another month. My food came out, the moment of a hundred Christmases. I took a bite, and my body lit up like the tree at Rockefeller Center. Never had a meal permeated every cell of my body like that, and it hasn't happened like that since. Life was good again. I was reborn.

This overwhelming feeling came over me. You mean I could tell myself yes again and be happy? I was almost proud of myself for doing something I wanted to do and not caring about anybody's approval. Every moment with that meal was a vacation. I couldn't let that feeling end. The only thing on my mind was where I was going to go next.

With the taste of grease and salt still on my lips, and a stomach that was fuller than it had been in months, I drove to another popular drive-through for dessert. Thinking I'd just get a vanilla cone to top off the feast I'd just had at the last restaurant (after all, my nickname is Two Scoops), I pulled into the drive through and saw a picture of a big burger with cheese and those crispy fries I'd loved since childhood. The intercom beeped on.

"Welcome! How are you today?"

"I'm having a fabulous night!" I said in a chipper tone.

"Awesome. How can I help you today?" she asked.

"I'll have a quarter pounder with cheese, a small fry, and a vanilla ice-cream cone."

"Will that be all for you tonight?" she asked, not knowing this was a repeat meal of the one I'd had just a few minutes ago.

"YES! That'll do it, thank you!"

I was beaming with joy with what felt like power and freedom. At the time, I was a size zero. At 5'10", I was damn near a bobble head. Always having been so active, I could put down some calories with the best of them, but I hadn't eaten anywhere near these many calories in one sitting since I'd been following the golden plan. With no problem, I shoved that burger, fries, and cone down and chased it with a pound of regret. I was stuffed. I was full all the way up to the top of my throat and was sure my stomach would explode. I couldn't sit down. All I could do was stand up and walk around, hoping the food would digest quickly and leave my body so I could get some sleep. I knew that if the natural process took too long, there was another option of throwing it up, but I most definitely wasn't going to do that. When the idea crossed my mind though, I realized just how unhealthy this whole thing had become. That wasn't who I was. I didn't want to go down that road that I knew would only lead to a whole new world of problems. I told myself this pain was what I deserved for making the decision I'd made. I should have stopped at the first meal, but I had spun out of control.

The next morning, my pores clogged up with salt and saturated fat and my emotions stuffed with disappointment, I had to look at my situation for what it was. I had gone overboard. I needed to balance physical health with mental health and recognize when things were becoming too much. I gave myself a pep talk and decided I wouldn't beat myself up about the previous day's decisions. It was a new day to make smarter choices, so that's what I did.

I never binged like that again because I never wanted to feel that way again, but I also learned how badly I needed to make decisions that would keep my head in a healthy place. All the interview practice, runway training, and nutrition plans in the world couldn't replace mental health.

I thought that since I was stretching my limits in new ways, I was exhibiting a growth mindset, but in reality, I was operating in a fixed mindset. If I didn't follow the plan to a T, I couldn't succeed. That wasn't true. While it's important to follow the guidelines of your trainers, it's also important to listen to your body and make adjustments as necessary. In a world with so much noise fighting for our attention, tapping into what your mind and body are telling you is the ultimate example of growth.

We have to make the best choices for the future we're creating. It will require some trial and error, but it's worth it to figure out what we need to attract in our lives for who we want to become. If your current decisions aren't pointing toward who you want to be in the long term, if they aren't making you a better person, and if your future self wouldn't thank you for today's decisions, it's time to make some adjustments.

Who is making the decisions for your life? What is influencing the person you desire to be? Do your decisions and mindset make you feel limited or empowered? Is your inner voice tuned to negative or positive self-talk?

To develop a positive sense of self and avoid making decisions that can lead you down dark roads, even if you started off with the best of intentions, use these guidelines to help determine if you're on the right path:

Do not speak anything out loud that will harm or degrade you. If you wouldn't say it to or appreciate it from somebody else, you shouldn't say it to yourself.

Surround yourself with people who align with the life you're inspired to live. Anybody who doubts the size of your dreams is projecting their shortcomings on you. Don't let that attitude cloud your vision.

Keep your morals and values high. Don't let the outside world determine your worth.

Protect your mental health and nurture it often.

If you're believing negative thoughts about your body, flip that sentiment and tell yourself, "I've been blessed with the most beautiful, healthy body." Recondition your mind using every tactic at your disposal. Write empowering beliefs where you can see them. Repeat them out loud. Keep telling yourself great things about yourself until you believe them. This life is yours. You decide what to believe. Do not hand that power over to somebody else.

Chapter 6

IT'S NOT A DIET, IT'S A LIFESTYLE

Our bodies carry us through life every day. If we don't learn how to care for our bodies, we set ourselves up for pain down the road. Part of becoming the best version of yourself is being in good physical health. When we think about health, the picture in our head is usually someone with a super toned body and a perfect complexion who's always eating natural foods, but that's not necessarily an accurate description of what health truly is. Fortunately, our culture has become more aware of additional areas of life that also need attention, such as mental and emotional health, daily habits, and the physical strength and flexibility of our bodies. That's why when I coach my clients, I emphasize what I believe are the four pillars to maintaining good health: nutrition, healthy habits, accountability, and movement.

Every part of our being relies on every other part to function at full capacity. If one area suffers, it will trickle into other areas too.

They're all intertwined. There are basic, foundational truths about health that everyone should implement into their lifestyles, from what we eat to how we manage our time. If you make habits out of this information, all those small daily actions will amount to changes no one will be able to overlook. Since nutrition is one of the areas with the most misinformation surrounding it, let's start there.

NUTRITION

Scroll through your social media on any given day and you'll see a new diet. You'll find people saying completely different things about health and nutrition and what's good for you and what's not. Some say intermittent fasting is great, some like protein shakes for two meal replacements a day, others say fast food burger joints, as long as it's not every day. Here's the truth: everyone just needs to stick to the basics and start creating a healthy lifestyle that works for them. Focusing on a crash diet can get the results you desire, but only temporarily.

Your body is a sophisticated machine that requires quality fuel. Just like you can't run a car with alcohol, your body can't run off of poor substitutes for real nutrition. When I started my pageant journey, I figured I would go into old school bodybuilder mode and fill up on grilled chicken and broccoli. While that did allow me to lean out, I was always hungry for something more.

Knowledge is power when it comes to nutrition. I had no idea about portion sizes or the types of food I should be eating at different times of the day until I hired a nutritionist and trainer. To maintain a nutritious diet, remember a few things. Full disclosure: I'm not a personal trainer, but I am a certified health coach, so what I'm about to say is backed by education.

Healthy, lean proteins are your friend. Some examples may include chicken, fish, or lean beef. If you're not a meat-eater, some options could include eggs, beans, tofu, and tempeh, to name a few.

Veggies are your other best friend. If you want to play it safe, stick with the greens, such as spinach, broccoli, asparagus, romaine, and kale.

And for the love of God, no matter what anybody tells you, healthy carbohydrates are a must. They provide a source of energy and other vitamins and nutrients for your body. Some of my favorite healthy carbs are sweet potatoes, quinoa, brown rice, and whole grain breads.

I'm a big foodie, so I love to try new restaurants and cuisines, which can sometimes make it challenging to stay healthy. However, as a whole, I stick to a leaner protein and more low glycemic than high glycemic foods. That means staying away from fried foods, white breads, and white rice, and choosing more spinach and healthy proteins. I'm not perfect; I do love my ice cream. But what's important is developing the knowledge of the right and wrong times to indulge in your favorite meals. If you're of age and enjoy a nice glass of vino or a cocktail, do your best to be intentional about not drinking late at night (especially with the wine), and make sure you're sneaking some waters in between your drinks. Alcohol majorly affects your sleep patterns, and any type of sugars late at night settle right there in your lower belly. Ladies, I know we don't like that. That also goes for fruits.

Yes, fruit is healthy, but the best time to eat the natural sugars is right after a workout to help you refuel your muscles, not right before bed. One of the most important things I ever learned when it comes to nutrition is the importance of the time you eat. I try not to eat carbs past 7:00 p.m. When I was training hard, it was 6:00 p.m. Keep in mind that starving yourself is never a good idea. When you do, your plan will backfire. Yes, you may lose weight immediately, but the second you go back to your old ways, the pounds will pile back on, so you might as well learn healthy habits along the journey. This might even save you from going on a burger and ice-cream binge. To save yourself from going hungry, I recommend eating six small meals a day.

And finally, I can't talk about nutrition without talking about water—it's key! Up to 60 percent of your body is water. I suggest taking your weight, dividing it in half, and drinking that number of ounces of water per day. If you weigh 150 pounds, that's seventy-five ounces of water you should be drinking daily. Start and end your day with water. The first thing that touches your lips in the morning is what you'll crave all day, so start training your mind and body now to hydrate and replenish.

HEALTHY HABITS

Ohhhh boy, do I have a lot to say about habits! Your success in life won't come from the one time each month you decide to bust some cardio; success comes from commitment to habits. You'll get to celebrate the big moments because of the small things you do each day. We all have different responsibilities and commitments. We also all have twenty-four hours. Your daily routines will determine the course of your life.

I start each morning the same way. I wake up and make the bed the second my feet hit the ground so I set the tone of success for the day. After that, I make my coffee, read devotions, write down my gratitudes, and visualize my goals. Then I hit the gym or go on a hike. Most of the time when I'm working out, I'm listening to a personal development or business podcast to get my mind right for the day. I'm very intentional about my mornings because they set the tone for the rest of the day.

Incorporating the habit of getting sunshine every day is also a key winning habit. It helps if you're living in a naturally sunny climate. Oftentimes, we can get so caught up in our day-to-day routine that we forget the importance of taking breaks. Yes, I am also guilty of this! The time when your habits get tested the most is when life throws you a curveball. What do you stick with and what goes to the wayside? Whatever falls short is the habit you need to work on strengthening the most. Personally, I keep my morning routine, but my workouts get lighter, my visualization times get shorter, and I find myself having to say no to more people in order to keep my mental peace. When times get hectic and life gets busy, I rely on the things that I know make me my best and keep my mental and emotional health at its highest. If you have a habit of people-pleasing, and you feel guilty when you say no to others when life gets busy, then it's time to strengthen that muscle and find a sense of breakthrough within yourself.

There are times when we have to be real and honest with ourselves about habits, and then there's a time to give yourself grace. We can all be our worst critics. At one point, I was being really harsh on myself and thought I had a problem with time management until I accepted that my way of doing things didn't need to be like everybody else's. I used to think good time management meant having a set schedule for everything that looked the same each day, but I just couldn't fit myself into a box like that. That strategy works for some people, but for someone like me, I have found the best plan to manage my time is to create the habit of being fully present in whatever I'm doing. For me, time management is more of a juggle than a balance.

I have a lot of dreams, a lot of visions, and a lot of energy, which means I can squeeze a lot in from the time I open my eyes at five thirty in the morning to the time I go to sleep around nine thirty at night. And you know what? That's when I feel like I'm living out my purpose.

I've also realized that however I plan my days, I need to keep the special ones sacred.

One year, our family took a trip to Hawaii to celebrate my mom's birthday. It was one of the most incredible trips we'd ever taken. For five days, we were in absolute paradise. We did family excursions, enjoyed the spa, had delicious food and drinks, laughed the nights away, and reminisced about old memories while daydreaming about the ones to come. It was a beautiful, special time. One other thing I remember about that trip is that up to that point in my career, that month had been the most lucrative.

Now, one thing you have to understand about me is my need for consistent habits. When I get out of my rhythm, it's extremely hard to get back in it. If I take a vacation, it takes me a couple days after that to get my head back in the game. 'Tis the struggles of being an all-or-nothing personality. I figured since I'd been crushing it professionally, I wanted to stay in that groove. I knew that if I completely unplugged for those five days, I'd be sacrificing another couple days after the trip because I wouldn't be able to dive right back in, so I didn't fully unplug.

I worked every morning before the family woke up, took calls when I felt like I needed to, and listened to my mentorship videos in the middle of the day. Even though I shut my phone off at six each evening, I was still putting in the hours to keep the momentum going in my business. When I think about it now, part of me wishes I would have planned things differently and been fully present there with my mom and the rest of my family. I was trying to figure out a healthy juggle, but it didn't go so well. When we all went our separate ways and I got home, I didn't even feel like I'd been on a vacation. I knew I needed to make some changes.

If you plan for it, you can do a little bit of work while you're on vacation. Other times, there's something to be said about setting the electronics aside. You're the only one who can decide what's best and when. I decided after that trip that if I committed to anything from then on, I would be there 100 percent. If I said I was going on vacation, having a girls night, having a date night, holding a coffee meeting, or enjoying some self-care or silent time by myself, I would be present where my feet were and with whoever was with me. A mentor said to me, "I'm always present with whoever I'm with. I'm not thinking about dinner, tomorrow's plans, going to the gym—nothing but being present in this conversation with you." Since then, I decided I wanted to live my life this way. If I can't be all-in present somewhere, I don't go at all. Life is precious, and every moment holds a memory of its own. So if you need to handle a few things for your life, your business or your future, find the time to do it when you can be the most present. Once you start taking on this motto, you'll cherish your time more and the memories will be much sweeter.

ACCOUNTABILITY

Accountability partner, say whaaat! Your daily habits can slip unless you don't have a form of accountability. Whether it's a friend, a coach, mentor, or an app that keeps you accountable, you'd best find yourself something!

When no one is watching and holding us accountable, it's easy to make excuses for ourselves, eat a little something here and there that isn't conducive to our goals (which ends up being several bites of a little something), skip a day of working out (which often ends up being more than one day), or keep putting off those little things that could amount to a major change in our career or business a year from now. We can justify to ourselves why we did or didn't do the things we said we were going to do. We pretend like our excuses are real because we don't have to answer to anybody but ourselves. But when we bring someone else into the mix who won't tolerate us settling for less than what we're capable of, we start to make real change.

People hire coaches, mentors, nutritionists, personal trainers, and other professionals for just this reason. They've tried to go at it alone, and they keep finding themselves at square one. I will keep saying it until I can't say it anymore: the people you surround yourself with make all the difference in your success. Find somebody who believes in you to hold you to your word. This person needs to challenge you to go higher, encourage you, be honest with you, and celebrate all your wins—big or small. You might be able to recruit a friend or family member for this, but if not, hiring someone to fill this role is more than worth the investment.

FITNESS

Everybody loves a good workout, right? Waking up at 5 a.m., going to the gym, sweating your butt off, every single morning, forever . . .

Said no one ever. We all know very few people like that. Most people do it because they know it's good for them. Your body is a machine. Just like if you park your car for months and it's slow to start, your body will be stiff and prone to injury if you don't move it on a daily basis. You don't have to work out like you're training for the Olympics, but it is healthy to move consistently. If you're looking for the perfect workout, it's whatever you like to do, because that's what you'll keep doing. It's good to mix things up once or twice a week, but as long as you're moving thirty minutes a day, you're on the right track. All those little things, like parking farther away from the door of the grocery store to get in more steps or taking the stairs instead of the elevator add up, too.

Be careful who you listen to about fitness. You don't have to subscribe to the "Go hard or go home! Beast mode!" way of doing things. If your body is telling you to stop, listen. When you need to rest, rest. When it's time to move, move.

SENSE OF FULFILLMENT

Feeling fulfilled is important. If you can't find what makes you feel alive and happy, then life is much more difficult to navigate. That's why I believe you need to do something every single day that fulfills you. It can be big or small, public or private. However you do it, make it part of your daily habits.

I know this is easier said than done, especially when some elements of your life are beyond your control. As far as it depends on you, curate your environment for joy. Cut out negative influences, habits, and environments. If you can't get rid of them all, dig deeper into the things that light you up. Personally, the beach is that thing for me. There's nothing like listening to the waves crashing in, feeling the breeze with the salty air, and soaking up the rays on a beautiful sunny day. I try to go to a beach as much as possible and enjoy sunrises and sunsets wherever I go. It rejuvenates my soul. Where is that place for you?

When a getaway isn't in the cards, be mindful to do things you can do anywhere. Meditate, breathe, get some fresh air, light your favorite candle, call your best friend or a family member. Anything that makes your heart happy, do that.

We can get so caught up in achievement that we forget to take special moments for ourselves. We forget that any day could be our last. Not to get morbid on y'all, but for real. Every day is a gift. Let's start acting like it. Start being intentional about putting your own mental and physical health first. You deserve it.

Chapter 7

QUITTING ISN'T AN OPTION

I remember the moment I broke out of the awkward teenage stage. As a kid, I had braces for three years. I don't mean the cute "girl next door" kind of braces. My jaw was crooked, and I had an overbite, so I had to sport the headgear, the rubber bands, the expander at the top of my mouth that I had to crank—the whole nine yards. I had so much equipment, I could supply an entire orthodontist's office. On top of that, I'd spent a big chunk of childhood with my brother and his friends playing ball, camping, and baiting the hook when we went fishing. Those things resonated with me more than dancing, cheerleading, and other typical "girly-girl" activities, but I still loved to wear cute outfits, so I always had a sweet spot for shopping.

I was sixteen years old, shopping on Chicago's Michigan Avenue with my mom, when an Abercrombie recruiter approached me.

"Hey, have you ever thought about modeling before? Because you definitely have what it takes to model for us."

I was caught way off guard, but heck yeah I was interested! That was the day my confidence got its booster shot.

While I didn't end up pursuing the Abercrombie opportunity, I did become interested in the world of modeling. About a year after the recruiter approached me, I went to a modeling agency in Omaha, Nebraska, not far from our home in Iowa. They said they wanted to interview me, so I went to a casting call. Talk about all dolled up—I put on the most fashion forward outfit I had, made sure my makeup was on point, and curled my hair to perfection. It was obvious that I didn't know much about the expectations of the industry. For a casting call, you're supposed to wear simple clothes, keep your hair soft and natural, and go easy on the makeup—way easy. Even still, they told me I had everything it took to be a successful model, and they were just the ones to launch my career. All I had to do was give them $2000.

It felt strange that they would ask me for that much money—any money—to get me started as a model. I did my research and figured out pretty quick that it was a scam. Legit agencies sign you, then take a percentage from the jobs they book for you. That agency was shady, which was unfortunate, but I was happy we figured that out sooner than later! Even though the deal was no deal at all, I realized at that moment that I had a deeper desire to bring out my inner girly-girl. I'd tried out for the dance team once and that had been an epic fail, so the extent of my experience in girly activities was my season as a Lil' Rams cheerleader for the youth football team at our school. I'll always remember the days when I was overlooked by the boys in middle school because I was a "late bloomer" and didn't have the big kahunas that every teenage boy was obsessed with. In high school the tables started to turn, but by then, I was so focused on sports and traveling in the summer that boys weren't at the top of my priority list. Still, all throughout high school and on into college, I continued to embrace more of my feminine side.

It was my first day on campus at the University of Iowa. I had just said my goodbyes to my parents as they headed back home four hours away. I sat there a little sad, but excited for the next chapter in my life. Everything was so new. In the middle of trying to figure out what was next, I did what any freshman in college would do: I started mindlessly scrolling through social media. All of a sudden, an ad popped up that said, "Compete for Miss USA!" My first thought was, There's no way I could do that, but something immediately kicked into my subconscious and said, "Yes, you can!" Momma is always my first phone call when I have something exciting to share, so I dialed her number. She answered the phone and said, "Do you want me to come back and pick you up?"

"Ha ha ha. Very funny, Momma. No, I'm calling because I just saw an ad talking about competing in Miss USA. Wouldn't that be cool? I mean, I don't know if I can do that," I said, hoping she'd disagree with me.

"What do you mean? You can do anything you put your mind to. Why don't you look into it? I believe in you, sweetie."

At that point, the decision was made.

I hung up the phone and started my research. Because I was eighteen, I applied for Miss Iowa Teen USA. I figured I'd stand a better chance of winning as the oldest competitor in the teen division instead of the youngest in the miss division. Thinking the process to enter would take a while, I sat back and waited to be notified. Not long after that, I got a letter in the mail that said, "Congrats! You're an official contestant for Miss Iowa Teen USA!" I only had two months to prepare, but I just knew I would crush it (or so I thought).

When you commit to something, there's always a sacrifice. I was a freshman in college. All I really wanted to do was eat burritos with queso and toasty garlic grilled cheese sandwiches with friends after a fun night out on the town. Instead, I was in the cafeteria eating chicken and broccoli every day and working out when I wasn't in class. When the pageant came around, I put on my sparkly pink gown, covered my body in spray tan, styled my hair all poofy, and painted on the best smokey eye stage makeup I could. I thought I was killing it. I was feeling good, ready to make my mark in the pageant world, but I didn't feel good for long; I ended up placing in the top fifteen out of about thirty contestants. Landing in the top half wasn't enough. Anything less than winning wouldn't have been enough. My family was excited, but I was disappointed. And hungry. All I wanted to do was eat something greasy and sugary, then go back to the drawing board to figure out my strategy for the next competition.

After reflecting, I decided to take the following year off, focus on college, and really figure out if this pageant thing was for me. Not long after I'd made that decision, I was approached by a pageant director for the Miss America Organization. They asked if I would be interested in competing at the local level. Keep in mind, I had just competed for a pageant in the Miss Universe Organization (MUO) at the state level, so for me to switch organizations and compete in a local pageant didn't really seem intriguing at the time. Ultimately, I ended up saying the heck with it—let's give it a try anyway. I didn't want to write it off. What if I turned out to love it or it turned out to lead to something amazing? I signed up.

The Miss America Organization (MAO) has a talent portion. Needless to say, I couldn't roll out a basketball hoop and shoot three-pointers, so I decided to play the piano. I signed up for a piano elective class in college to force myself to practice every week. My piano teacher helped me pick a song and practice it until it was as perfect as it was going to get. Then came pageant weekend.

There were only seven girls competing. When I arrived, the event organizers took us to a basement, a dark dungeon that smelled like cow manure. This is where I had to get dressed in my fancy evening gown? Lord help us all. Before long, the competition started, and it was my turn to go present my talent. They wheeled this old wooden piano onto the stage. It was uncomfortably silent in the room, but in my mind, it was game time. I looked out into the audience and saw my parents beaming with joy. I started playing my song, and as I kept going, I kept hitting keys that weren't working. Instead of moving on and pretending like nothing was wrong, I just kept my finger on that note and pounded it until it worked. Well it never did. I'd hit another key. Broken. No noise. By this time, my song was completely butchered. My mom slowly sank down in her seat. No song has ever lasted as long as that song seemed to last that day, and I'd never failed at something so miserably, ever. I finally got through the song, but boy was it terrible. Even though there was nothing I could have done about the broken keys, I was still humiliated. I'd just made a fool of myself in front of the entire audience on a stage that smelled like cow manure in Small Town, USA. So not to my surprise (or anybody else's), I didn't even make the top three. That day was a supersized serving of humble pie.

At the age of twenty-one, I decided the Miss USA Organization was more my style. No talent portion. Hallelujah. I competed for Miss Iowa USA and placed as a semifinalist, top fifteen. Things weren't looking very promising for my pageant career. Maybe I was better off just sticking to sports. I had hired a runway coach, so I felt confident in my walk and posing. I'd hired an interview coach, so I felt great about that, too. But I couldn't figure out why I wasn't at least placing in the top five. My family was supportive through it all, but I was doubting the process. This time, I went through with the plan to take a year off.

I sat down and reflected on why I wasn't placing higher. I'd created all these stories in my head. Maybe I'm not the right age. Maybe this is just a business. Maybe they want somebody with a different hair color . . . personality . . . cut of evening gown. I would tell myself anything to avoid admitting that I just wasn't the best yet and needed to dig in and do the work. During my year off, I hired coaches and mentors who resonated better with my vision for myself and what I wanted out of pageantry. I figured that if I was going to keep doing this, spending my time and resources on this dream, then I needed to go all out. I spent those two years learning, studying, listening, practicing, interviewing, and giving it everything I knew to give. Like my coach always said, I left no stone unturned.

In the meantime, I graduated from the University of Iowa and moved to St. Louis to sell commercial flooring (glamorous, right?!). When I got to Missouri, I got the pageant bug again. I continued with the stories in my head, but this time they were a little different. It's a new state. There will be new directors, new judges. It's a fresh start. What do I have to lose? If I don't try, I won't know. I'd done the work and prepared for two years. I was more confident in who I was as a person, I'd graduated, and I'd worked on everything the pageant would throw at me. I was ready to be the next Miss Missouri USA. The day of the pageant came. I placed as a semifinalist again.

By now, I was starting to get frustrated. What was there left to do? It was time to look at this thing from a new perspective. Why did I want to win? Why did I feel the need to keep competing? What was on the other side of that crown that I was so willing to keep fighting for?

When we're not winning or getting the results we want, we start questioning the process. That's when we need to lean in the most. It was then that I realized—during times of transition, when you're chasing a dream that only seems to run away from you the more you want it, you need to take a moment and get real with yourself. You can either go deeper than you ever have before, or you can pack up and move on to something else. I decided that I was going to go big. It was Miss USA or bust.

Before then, I'd hired mentors and coaches, but this time, I hired an expert for each division of the competition. It was time to seriously invest in myself and my future. I hired a current events coach, an interview coach, a runway coach, a nutritionist and trainer, and two former Miss USAs. My motivation for winning had changed. I wanted to win because I knew it would give me a platform. That platform would give me influence. With influence, I could teach women how not to give up when everything is telling them they should. I knew my calling was to walk them through the process of overcoming the challenges in their lives, infuse them with confidence, and use my story and experiences as examples of how to persevere. If I was going to teach women that giving up wasn't an option, it couldn't be an option for me, either. By being Miss Missouri USA, and ideally Miss USA, that influence could be nationwide. I would show women, and all people for that matter, that it's worth it to keep going.

I went back and competed again. That year, more prepared than ever, I got second runner-up. Even though I didn't win the crown and sash, I was proud of myself because I was getting closer to the results I wanted, and the judges were starting to recognize that. Knowing what I'd done to get to that point, I was sure that when I returned the following year, the crown would be mine. I had made the training process my lifestyle, not just a few-months cramming session. The next year, more prepared and confident, I stood on the stage, hand-in-hand with one last competitor, waiting to hear my name as they announced the new Miss Missouri USA. With suspense flowing through the auditorium, the emcee called the other girl's name. I'd placed first runner-up. That year was, by far, the most difficult. I was so close to winning the crown, I could taste it. By then, I had competed five times at the state level for MUO. I didn't understand. I could only chalk it up to God's timing.

There's no way I could get that close and not go for it one more time. But trust me, I had my doubts. Again, questions started to pop up about whether this was actually for me. I figured there was only one thing that I hadn't done, one area of my life where I was "settling." My career. I wasn't being fulfilled by my sales position. I trusted that God had other plans.

On more occasions than I can count, random people would come up to me and say I should be a sports reporter. I mean, all the time, all over the country, on planes, in restaurants, shopping—you name it, people would tell me this. They'd say I had the perfect voice, and it probably also helped that I was outgoing and enjoyed talking with others. When I'd tell them I loved sports as well, they'd say it was the perfect fit. I already knew how to perform in front of people because of basketball and pageantry, and let's be real, I've never seen a microphone I didn't love! After some time, I figured these strangers might be onto something. If they were right, I wouldn't want to miss out on such an awesome opportunity. The more I thought about it, the more I wanted to pursue sports reporting, but I didn't have any connections in the industry. I said to myself, What if I just did it? What if I just took a chance? Where would I go? Would I still be able to come back one more year and compete at Miss Missouri USA? How could I make two dreams come true at the same time?

Shortly after all of these thoughts came to mind, I was talking to one of my high school besties, Lydia, who was a travel nurse at the time. It just happened to be that she and her friend Ashley's next rotation was in Los Angeles, which was also the number two market for sports reporting. Hello, all the connections in the world! The wheels in my head started turning. I had to go for it. I quit my sales job on a whim, packed up a small rental trailer truck, secured an extended rental apartment in the heart of Hollywood, and fired off to LA. In a moment of complete uncertainty, we Midwesterners were off to the big city! After living in three different rentals in seven months, networking my tail off in the sports reporting world, taking endless TV and hosting courses, and modeling full-time, I discovered the unexpected: what's more important than winning is who you're becoming in the process.

I fell in love with the energy and opportunities that Los Angeles provides. People move out there to chase dreams. Literally living on a prayer. But soon, my time was up in LA and I went back home to Missouri to pursue my other dream. Pageant weekend came and I'd never felt more ready. Everything was aligned. Not because I had been training vigorously, but because I was living and being the titleholder every day. That year when pageant weekend came around, my coaches told me to walk through the door knowing I was there to pick up my crown. "This year, it belongs to you," they said. I had an unexpected confidence boost that year because I had finally discovered who I was through the journey and didn't have to fake it any longer.

It was down to the last two minutes of competition, and the winner was about to take the crown. Once again, I was one of the last two girls standing. Adrenaline rolling, heart pounding out of my chest, talking to God every step of the way, I heard the emcee say the words I'd been waiting years to hear.

"The young woman who wins tonight will advance to compete in our national pageant, Miss USA 2018. Our Miss Missouri USA 2018 isss . . . (insert the longest three seconds my life) . . . TORI KRUSE!!!!!!!!

Holy crap, I FREAKING DID IT!!!!! The moment I'd prayed for, worked my butt off for, sacrificed for, stayed up late for, cried for, overcome doubts for—it'd all paid off! There's no better feeling in the world than winning something you've worked so dang hard for. The second I won, I pointed up at God and said "Thank you!" I had visualized that moment for so many years, I felt like I'd been there before. My heart had never been so happy, so happy that the second they placed the crown and sash on me, I walked away without the flowers to run over to my family and blow them kisses. They were in tears, beaming with happiness. I couldn't wait to run off that stage and hug them. My ride or dies. My biggest fans through everything. Overwhelming gratitude flowed through my veins. I was so proud of myself for never giving up.

Now it was on. The journey to Miss USA. A moment I'd dreamed of since sitting in my dorm room freshman year eight years before. Winning the crown took a tremendous amount of perseverance when it would have been easier to hang up my heels. But each time, I got back on my feet, reevaluated my team of coaches, and picked apart every single element of my performance to figure out what worked and what didn't. I stepped into the unknown. I got uncomfortable. When I trained, I was always training for the levels above me. When it came to hiring experts to work with, I refused to hire anyone who didn't believe I could be Miss Universe. Every day when I woke up, I wondered to myself, "What is Miss USA doing today?" If I didn't think Miss USA would be doing something I was about to do, I wouldn't do it, because in my head, that crown was already mine. I became obsessed with the process and had to mentally put myself in positions before I was there physically.

Representing Missouri was one of the best years of my life. It was an honor to be chosen and trusted with that responsibility. To have my name attached to a state and hold that type of influence was something I took very seriously. My success didn't come overnight, which made me appreciate it even more. I vowed to myself that I would never take a moment like this for granted. I wanted to be the best representative I could possibly be. I wanted to make Missouri proud and make the most of the experience because I knew I only got one year as Miss Missouri USA and one chance at becoming Miss USA. The title was incredible, but it was the people who came along the ride with me that made being a titleholder so memorable, especially my mom, my #1 fan, my built-in manager or "Mommager." From endless parades to Veterans Day celebrations, speaking at schools, and news appearances, my momma was there for it all, and I couldn't have done half of that without her love and support. When it came to Miss USA, I remember every moment, including the ever-so-lovely early mornings and long rehearsals. In the moments when I was tired of being "on," I'd remind myself that there was some girl, if not many, who wished she was in my shoes, so I'd better suck it up, stop complaining, and cherish every second I spent in that once-in-a-lifetime opportunity. The year I competed at Miss USA, it was held in Louisiana. We were there for ten days making multiple appearances. We had police escorts everywhere, and the cameras were always rolling, things I was definitely not used to back home in Missouri. We couldn't even leave our rooms without a security guard. I had to be on top of my game at all times, and it was still the best moment of my life that I got to spend with fifty other high-achieving women. It was all surreal.

Forty-two family members and friends traveled to Louisiana to cheer me on. Forty. Two. It's still unbelievable to me. Heck, I didn't know I had that many friends! I turned twenty-seven while I was at

Miss USA, and on my birthday, I filmed a video during a break to individually thank every person who came to support me. My mom played it at the big family and friends dinner that evening. My brother called me right after he watched it and said he was bawling like a baby because he was so proud. Although that gave me a good laugh the night before prelims, it also made me realize that the brother/sister bond Trav and I share is unbreakable.

Was that video convenient to make? No. I was filming myself in our hospitality suite, crying every other word through my fake lashes and loads of foundation as other contestants walked in staring at me like I was an emotional nitwit. But I did it and stopped caring what other people thought. Sometimes you have to make choices that may seem inconvenient at the time, or you may look like an idiot to someone else, but the effect your efforts have on others is ten times more important and worth every second. At that moment, I realized that life's greatest treasures are the people you're surrounded by.

You can't go through life waiting on everything to be perfect. Take the uncomfortable steps, go the extra mile, love on the people who mean the most to you, and hold your dreams close. It may just lead you to the life you've always wanted.

Chapter 8

STOP WAITING— CREATE IT YOURSELF

Fear holds us back from our greatest desires. Remember when I said I moved to LA to pursue sports reporting once I placed first runner-up? Let me tell you a little bit more about that. The closer I got to winning Miss Missouri USA, the more I realized that God was calling me to more. Two things were constantly at the forefront of my mind: winning the next year's pageant, and seeing if people were right when they assured me I'd make a good sports reporter. One I'd be tweaking; the other, I'd be starting anew. I had no experience with reporting, but I was ready to try. The year I placed first runner-up, I was devastated for two reasons: I'd lost, of course, but if I wanted to go for the crown again, I would have to leave Missouri for somewhere with more TV opportunities. I couldn't go—I WAS SO CLOSE! I sucked it up and decided to hold off on the second dream until after I'd made the first one come true.

That decision didn't last long. I couldn't get it out of my mind. I talked to my coaches about it and realized I didn't have to stay in Missouri during the "off season;" that's why we have short-term rental apps. I made the hard decision to quit my sales job. It was hard because I didn't want to put a damper on the relationship with the family friend who'd given me the opportunity, and I never want to feel like a quitter. Ultimately, I decided the best thing to do was leave them in a position to be successful and move on. That way, we'd all win.

I started my search to find the best city in the United States to pursue reporting, which I'd be doing while I trained for my next pageant. I kept my residency in St. Louis and moved out to Los Angeles, even though some people tried to talk me into starting off small, but I was ready to go straight to the top!

I took to heart what people were saying about me being a reporter. I just knew it would be a great fit. My pageant interview experience had set me up to be in front of thousands of people, asking and answering questions, keeping the audience engaged. I slowly began to gather the confidence I needed, but I knew I wasn't at the top of my game, so in true Tori fashion, I invested in the best hosting expert I could find in LA to learn the craft. I did everything she said to do in training. I met other people who had their sights set in the same direction and eagerly made connections with people in all different areas of reporting.

Because of networking, I gathered some of the best advice anybody has ever given me. My friend Nikki introduced me to her friend Richie who worked for ESPN in LA. We got together for coffee, and he ended up being a tremendous mentor. Had it not been for Miss Missouri, I wouldn't have met the choreographer who connected me to him. One day at coffee, Richie said, "I know you're new, but people who've been in the industry for years appreciate when newcomers are hungry to succeed. They're more willing to help than you might think. Here's what you should do: go on social media and connect with everybody in the industry you can think of. Introduce yourself, thank them for the connection, mention that you're new to the industry and what your goals are, and ask if they'd be willing to give five minutes of their time to offer you some advice.

Every day, I went on a professional social media platform and added as many people as it would let me. Every day, I hit the limit. Once the people accepted my connection, I'd do what my mentor had instructed me to. That one action got me more than fifty calls and meetings with people in the industry. I felt like I'd hit the lottery.

I was getting the connections, but there was one thing I needed that I still didn't have: experience. You need experience to get better opportunities, but you can't get experience unless you already have experience. I knew just how to fix that. Off I went to a party supply shop to buy a grassy carpet. I connected a microphone to my cell phone and put it on a tripod. I spent my weekends watching games on TV and taking notes. Once the games were over, I'd put on my reporter dress, complete with hair and makeup, and record myself reporting on whatever game I'd just watched. After I'd done this enough times, I put all the videos into my computer's movie creator and made a highlight reel.

Boom. Experience. Let's Go!

I sent the highlight reel to the sports hiring manager of one of the most popular news platforms in the country and waited. Not long after that, he called me and asked if I could meet with him. I couldn't say yes quickly enough. The reporting scenarios I'd painted in my head were unfolding before my eyes. When I pulled into the parking lot of the studio, I sat in my car and took a video. "This time next year, I'll be on the sidelines," I told the camera.

I was just as grateful for the opportunity to meet that hiring manager as I was proud of myself for taking such a bold step. I didn't get hired, but I had gathered connections and built relationships with many of them. I kept doing my highlight reels and looking for the next opportunity.

The Special Olympics have always held a special space in my heart, so I connected with the organization in Southern California and asked if they'd like me to be a sports reporter for their summer games. They loved the idea and we made it happen. Did I know what I was doing? Oh no, far from it! But it was fun and it was more experience. I just had to keep creating my own opportunities until something clicked.

Two of my former mentors, Shandi and Susie, who had both held the title of Miss USA, saw my potential and drive. They knew that if I didn't know something, I would figure it out. They, too, saw reporter potential in me and helped me create a plan to go after it. Being the out-the-box thinkers they were, they gave me the idea to go to a Hawkeyes game and interview tailgaters.

Not long after they gave me that idea, I grabbed my phone and microphone, dressed like a sports reporter, wrote questions on a piece of paper, and went around the university with my mom during the Iowa vs. Michigan game to interview tailgaters. Whether I looked like an idiot or not, I don't know, but I didn't care. I was determined. Doing something big requires taking big risks and looking like a newbie while you do it. When I had my vision in mind, what people thought about me didn't matter. I combined the film from that day with my highlight reel and kept moving toward my dream.

In the meantime, I met with someone who worked for a college sports network. Since my alma mater was part of that network, I was beyond excited to learn all I could about the organization. I attended the annual sports luncheon and they gave me a walkthrough of their headquarters in Chicago, giving me the opportunity to see what my future would look like if I pursued this path. I asked questions, learned all I could, and got to see firsthand that people who are already living your dream want to help you get there, too. They appreciate your grind if they've been in your shoes. The network appreciated my highlight reel as much as the last company, but that wouldn't be my final stopping point, either.

I kept looking and found a position with a freelance sports company in L.A. They hired me to develop my own sports stories and report them online. All that time I was making my highlight reels in the living room of my rental apartment, I'd been training for this job without knowing it. The dots were starting to connect, but I couldn't stay there long.

It was getting close to time to go back and compete. I'd been training for Miss Missouri USA the whole time, but more importantly than that, I'd learned so much about myself, perseverance, practice, hard work, and how to create my own opportunities before the decision makers had a chance to offer them. Little did I know the confidence I gained from those experiences was pageant training, too.

That was the year I won. I'm convinced the reason I won is that I knew who I was and had already done the work to prove myself before I was the titleholder. I didn't need the crown to be the fullest version of myself; the crown would only be an addition. Today, when competitors ask me how to prepare for the interview, I tell them when the judges ask them why they would make a great titleholder, they need to be able to tell them what they've achieved during the process. Same with a job interview. You have to walk into that meeting with your employer ready to discuss your experiences. When you do that, it shows that you're a go-getter, not a talker. You put action to your words, with or without the job.

My entrepreneurial spirit and desire to influence the masses led to an initiative I named "1st ManUp." Since I was so close to my brother, I related more to the "bros" than I did the "chicks." I went around to middle and high schools and spoke to young men about sexual harassment, preventing sexual assault, and respecting women. The energy was great. After I shared a speech, I'd ask, "Who will you be?" and they'd stand and respond, "1st ManUp!" My reach was expanding. Because I'd laid the groundwork, I was getting the chance to make a positive difference as a titleholder.

After those assemblies, young guys would tell me how their girlfriends had previously been in abusive relationships or how they struggled with low confidence and wanted advice on how to handle it. At times I almost didn't feel qualified, but I knew God was putting me in this position for a reason. By the time I finished my year as Miss Missouri USA, I'd started my speaking and coaching business. My nine-year pageant journey had led to this. Without a doubt, those nine years were the most developmental time in my life. I discovered who I was, had great leadership opportunities, and proved to myself that I could overcome obstacles and get back up stronger every time.

When you step out of your comfort zone, God will reward you for it. It's an act of faith. You'll prove it to yourself, improve your skills, and show the people around you what you're capable of. Don't be afraid to think bigger than you ever have before. If the door isn't open, create your own.

Chapter 9

SMALL HABITS LEAD TO BIG RESULTS

You'd think that after years of sports and competition, I'd have had the ins and outs of routines figured out from the get-go, but let me let you in on a little secret: I didn't even know about routines until about 2015 when I decided to get serious about my pageant journey. Before that, I went through the motions, listened to the instructions of my coaches, rode life's waves, and did what I needed to do to scratch items off my to-do list each day. After learning the advantages of morning routines via Michael Strahan's Wake Up Happy, where he describes his routine minute by minute, I decided to design one for myself. If I wanted to win, I would have been crazy not to create a routine. Let me tell you why.

Nobody just wakes up one day, orders what they want out of life, and has it delivered on their doorstep. It would be nice, but it doesn't work that way. Successful people orchestrate their success by planning the days, hours, and minutes. What they do in those minutes, hours, and days equates to their life. I did a little digging to see if morning routines were a common denominator of successful people, and SURPRISE—they are! The mindset they establish when they first wake up preps them to win the day. When I found out that the most successful leaders get up around 5:00 a.m., write down their goals for the day, work out, write down their gratitudes, and visualize their winning moments, they manifest their desires. They're not lucky; they're prepared by being intentional with their schedules. I wanted to be intentional, so I created my own morning routine.

I aim to go to bed no later than 9:30 p.m. so I can get up at 5:30 a.m.

I wake up, make my bed, light a candle, drink coffee, and read my devotionals

Journal time. Part of my journaling process is writing a thank-you to God (a.k.a. gratitudes). I focus on thanking God for ten different things for that day. When you do this, your brain begins to subconsciously look for the good in the day. Sometimes, my list might include running water, toothpaste, my car that gets me from point A to B, the breath in my lungs, or the pen to write with in my notebook. It doesn't matter how basic the thing I'm grateful for seems. In fact, the smaller the better, because it trains me not to overlook small miracles or take what I consider normal for granted. Once your brain is programmed to look for the small things, you begin to rewire the natural negativity in your brain that we're all born with. After that, what used to rile you up won't really matter anymore. Your complaints will start to fade away, and that positivity will spill over into every area of your life.

Last, I write out my goals, which don't all stay the same each day. I don't just list them either; I write them out like they've already happened as "I am" statements. For example, instead of saying, "I want a beach house," I write, "I AM the owner of our home in Hawaii." "I am speaking on Tony Robbins's stage." "I am married and have a beautiful family." "I am the owner of a charity that helps impoverished children." Try it out and watch how you start to manifest your dreams and they no longer seem so out of reach.

Once you've read something that connects you to God or The Spirit, take a moment to write down what you're grateful for, hash out your "I am" statements, and follow through with whatever else comprises your morning routine (meditation, movement, etc.). If there's a lot on your mind, it can help to dump your thoughts onto paper. This exercise gets your creative juices flowing and gets the "stuff" off your mind that might be blocking your positivity or creativity. Sometimes when I'm irritated or upset, instead of talking about my frustrations or complaining, I write it out of me.

James Clear, author of the book Atomic Habits, says if you have a hard time staying disciplined with an activity you'd like to make part of your routine, pair it with something you do all the time. For example, when I finish my morning writing, I go to the gym. This was my groove for four years. Even still, sometimes, you just won't feel like getting up early or you won't have time. That is okay. Some days, the most spiritual thing you can do is listen to what your mind and body are telling you they need. When you're too rigid, what should give you energy can feel like a chore. Make sure that you're mentally present when you perform these activities and that you're not just doing them as a checklist, because then they become worthless. If you build up too much resistance against these activities that are meant for good, you run the risk of falling out of your habits altogether. There are times you may wake up late or miss parts of your routine for some other reason, but don't let that throw you all out of whack. Just ask yourself how you can conquer the day from that point forward, tee yourself up for success, and go for it.

I've had times in my life when I was disciplined to the point of obsession. Grace? What was that? Grace wasn't gonna put a sash across my chest, but the daily grind was. That attitude pushed me toward some major positive places, but also some mentally and emotionally draining ones. Now that I know better, I do better. If I have to pray while I'm in the shower or making my bed, it's all good. Do what you can with what you have and watch your small efforts add up to big results.

Speaking of small efforts, think about the things you do that might not get much thought because they're so habitual. For example, how many hours a day do you sit? Think about the hours you spend at school or work. Are you at a desk most of the day? Are you staring at a computer all that time? Sitting excessively can lead to unnecessary weight gain, illnesses like heart disease, back problems, and anxiety[4]. Staring at a computer for hours can give you a headache. If you're sitting down and looking at a computer all day, get your booty up and move!

It's easy to sit in a chair for hours without even realizing it. Set your timer for once an hour so you can take a short walk, stretch, or do deep-breathing exercises. If you can, go outside and soak in the sunshine for five minutes. When I was in college, I'd go outside between classes to a beautiful space on campus to rejuvenate my brain. Breaks don't have to be long for their benefits to be tremendous.

There are twenty-four hours in a day, and some of us try to use all twenty-four of them. High achievers have a hard time turning it off. Our brains are always going, from the time we wake up to the time we pass out at night (and sometimes even while we're asleep). When we're

---

4   https://www.webmd.com/fitness-exercise/ss/slideshow-sitting-health

not in the office, we're thinking of how to get better at our jobs or grow our businesses. There's no such thing as clocking out; our minds won't let us. To this day, this is still my biggest challenge.

For entrepreneurs, students, or employees with heavy work-loads, it's hard to switch from work mode to any other mode, but if you don't learn to do it, you're setting up your relationships and your own mental health for disaster. There is a time and place to put in extra time for a launch or big event, but making it your everyday norm may leave you feeling overexerted or burned out.

Part of your winning routine should also include a form of rest, which won't look the same for everyone. Rest doesn't always have to be a day on the couch binging on your favorite movie. During the week, I plan at least one fun activity. I might go out for dinner, attend a sporting event, hit some golf balls at the range, or enjoy an afternoon at the pool. I find something to break the monotony of the work/eat/sleep cycle. Most people save these outings for the weekend, but I believe in enjoying life every day, not just Saturday and Sunday. You can hack the "living for the weekend" feeling by injecting some major fun into your week. One of my mentors noticed this and said, "You get a lot done, but one thing I love about you is that you know how to have fun!" That used to make me feel guilty, but now I'm proud of it because it keeps my mindset in a much healthier place. Don't go through your life counting down the hours on the clock. Create something to look forward to at a time when your psyche doesn't really expect it. You'll be surprised at how much lighter your life gets. Once you're done with all this work and fun, you need to make sure you're getting enough sleep.

I've listened to some personal development gurus before tell me that I only need 5.5 hours of sleep per night, but I tried that and it's a bunch of bologna. I get a non-negotiable 7.5–8 hours of sleep every night unless something wildly unordinary happens. If I get less than my seven, I feel like I can't log in to part of my brain. We exert so much energy all day long, we have to give our minds and bodies time to reload. Even if you're working all day, you're exerting more energy than you probably realize, mentally and physically. Sleep is important to recharge and refuel. If you want to be your best, you have to get your rest. I'm preaching to all of us who are tempted to do "just a little bit more" before bed, but that little more might be the culprit of our lack of quality sleep. Find pockets throughout your day to unplug. Go for a walk outside, close your laptop and take deep breaths, or take some time to stretch. These small actions will leave you less dependent on only your nighttime hours for rejuvenation.

If you're anything like me, when you turn in for the night, your body might be ready for rest, but that doesn't mean your mind always is. If your mind is racing when you should be asleep, or if you're in a state of high stress or high anxiety, relax with meditation music. Relaxation oils such as lavender and eucalyptus also help with winding down. Light candles for some dim light, and you're on your way to feeling like a million bucks.

When you're always moving, you might feel like you're operating at a high level, but your body can only do so much. Push yourself, do the necessary work to hit the goals you've set out for yourself, but don't "grind" so hard that you're leaving your emotional well-being behind. Don't leave your loved ones behind, either.

Take a moment to decide what's most important to you. This all comes down to how you define success. If I build a Fortune 500 company but I sacrifice all the time with my family, friends, God, and other important relationships, who's going to be there with me to share those wins? No one. Talk about a lonely life. A dollar sign is absolutely part of success. Money can provide the exact lifestyle and opportunities you dream of, but it's only a fraction of success. Maintaining healthy relationships is at the forefront. Could you imagine flying on your private plane with just you and the pilot because you don't have any friends to go with you? That's a depressing thought! So make sure your habits and routines also include life's most precious "success secrets." Make your routine with the important people in your life in mind.

Be intentional about how you spend your moments. Do an audit of how you spend your minutes and make adjustments wherever you need to. Winning routines don't end after your morning routine. Plan your days and watch your plans unfold.

Chapter 10

YOU'RE A WALKING BILLBOARD

Meeting new people is my jam! So is branding, networking, and pretty much anything social. Part of the reason for that is that I'm an extrovert. I thrive around people with positive energy. I crave new experiences and human interaction; it lights me on fire. Since I don't mind talking to anybody no matter where I am, I have made lasting connections in the most unexpected situations.

If networking were a state, I'd love to be the governor. In fact, one of my mentors calls me the Networking Maven. I do this because I know on some level, we're all connected. People's stories are captivating all on their own. When I hear about where they're from and how that's influenced the way they see the world, what they do each day, their areas of expertise, what makes them tick, their wildest dreams, it ignites something inside of me. So, when I sense one part of one person's story intertwining with someone else's—BOOM—connection time! Through the years, watching my parents as entrepreneurs, competing in sports and pageantry, and running my business, I've seen that what they say is true: you are a walking billboard.

FASHION & STYLE

When you play sports, they tell you to always be mindful of the way you act in public because you represent your school, your team, your family, and yourself. It's true! If you're wearing a sweatshirt with your university's name on it, you're representing that school. The same rules apply in every aspect of your life. If you look like you just rolled out of bed when you arrive at the airport, professionals look at you differently. Like it or not, people do judge books by their covers, but you don't have to see that as a bad thing. If you know people will hold on to their impression of you based on what they see, give an impression that you're proud of. While you're at it, realize you're not doing it for them. You're doing it for you.

Growing up, it was a family value to look nice wherever we went (except when we were camping). My mom bought me cute outfits when I was a kid because she wanted to make sure I felt good. Did she hit the nail on the head every time? Not every time, but mostly. There may or may not be a few holiday photos somewhere in a box of me wearing a questionable Christmas dress or matching family sweater, but other than that, I was dressed for success. As I grew older, I subconsciously took that lesson with me everywhere.

When I played basketball in high school, the team rule was to dress up during the day of home games. Me being me, I didn't want to just dress nice—I wanted to go a step above what was expected of us. Some classmates might have interpreted this as me wanting to show off, but it wasn't about that at all. You know the saying, "Dress for the job you want, not the job you have"? What do professional athletes do? They dress to the nines on game day. They always look like they spent just as much time with their stylist as they did with their strength coach. They walk into the arena or stadium like they're headed into New York Fashion Week. Part of this is for fashion, but a bigger part of it is psychological. When you look good, you feel good, and when you feel good, you play good. On top of that, people know you mean business.

My mom dressing me up as a kid and my coach setting the wardrobe standard for gameday are why it's second nature for me to show up ready for action now. From a young age, I understood that wherever I went, I represented everything I stood for. It doesn't matter if I'm on a plane, out to eat, at the gym, in a coffee shop, or heading to a wedding; when I show up, people know I take myself seriously, which suggests I'll take them seriously, too. Billboards don't talk, but they get your attention.

Dressing to impress isn't just about your confidence. You never know who you're about to meet when you walk out your door. When I travel, I plan on meeting my next client or the person who'll shake my hand at the end of my next business deal. I plan to cross paths with that dream connection I've been praying to meet. You won't catch me in an airport or restaurant looking like I just rolled out of bed. You can never lose by freshening up before you walk out the door.

Now, let me be clear. I love fashion! I can wear a dress one day or I can wear Jordan sneakers the next. My style doesn't mean your style. If you have different tastes, you do you! You don't have to be up on the latest ensembles to be well put-together. Wear something that makes your personality shine through. When you choose your outfit for the day, make sure you're proud to wear it and you feel good in it. If you ran into your dream connection, would you stand tall or shy away from them because of what you're wearing? First impressions are real and can set the stage for incredible things to happen in your future. Set yourself up for a win.

Your appearance is an element of manifestation. It's a signal to the universe that you are prepared to meet the client, employer, partner, or connection you've been preparing for. Who is it that you'd love to run into today who would help you level up? You don't know where they're going to be. Paths cross all the time. Don't let your big moment catch you off guard!

NETWORKING

During my pageant days, one thing I remember most is focusing on sitting next to someone new. Whether it was during rehearsals, during mealtimes, or on the bus going back-and-forth to the auditorium, my goal was to sit next to someone I'd never met before. I did this for two reasons. One, I always wanted to make the newbies feel comfortable. Since I'd been competing for a while, I'd find them to make them feel like they belonged in that environment. Two, it would take some of the stress off of me for competition. Every time you aim your focus on helping someone else, it removes the pressure from yourself. I'd ask them all about what their passions were, where they were from, and their reasons and goals for competing. Doing this would put the whole competition into perspective. We were there for a little while, but how we made each other feel would last for a lifetime. You never know how much you can impact someone's life just by asking simple questions. The comparison game can really get you if you're not careful. One way to remove the awkward factor with others is to get to know people's hearts. I still do that today if I start comparing myself to someone else or when intimidation starts to creep in. Instead of creating stories in my head about them, I go meet them and learn their real story. It relieves comparison and jealousy. It humanizes the person. We're all in this life together, so always give people the benefit of the doubt

Connecting with people is a value I hold dear. I've attended networking events since as long as I can remember because I know the value of meeting other people and making connections. The year I was Miss Missouri, I heard about The Global Beauty Awards, an award show that celebrates the pageant and beauty industry. The very first year of the award show, my mom and I flew to Washington to attend. When we walked in, we stepped into a networking wonderland.

You know I didn't go empty-handed. Business cards? Check. Elevator pitch? Check. Wardrobe? Come on, now. At this point in my life, I still wanted to be a sports reporter. I noticed that one of the women who was up for an award was the CEO of a sports management company. When I spotted her at the front table, I shot my shot. Something in me said, "Just go introduce yourself." I was super nervous. Being an extrovert doesn't cancel out the basic biology of intimidation. Luckily, my mom was there to encourage me. "This is your chance, Tori. Don't miss this opportunity." So I went for it.

I walked up and sat down in the empty chair right next to this powerful CEO. I introduced myself, handed her my business card, and made small talk. She was friendly and easygoing and made me feel so welcomed. I went back to my table soon after so we could both enjoy our night. Fast forward five years, I was presented the opportunity to host my own female empowerment mastermind alongside the award show, and that same powerful female CEO became one of the keynote speakers at my mastermind. It just goes to show, you never know what will happen when you step out of your comfort zone. I wouldn't be where I am today without my good friend and mentor Maureen, who made all of this happen. Just take one step at a time and the pieces will soon come together.

God always has a plan. Believe in it.

PUTTING YOURSELF IN THE RIGHT PLACE AT THE RIGHT TIME . . .

One of my favorite things to do is to take myself out for dinner. I'm not a loner, I swear. Taking yourself out to dinner provides that space for you to reflect on your life without any other opinions around you. I typically choose a nice place and sit at the bar because one, I love great food, and two, you never know who you might run into at a nice restaurant. Put yourself in the right places so you can attract opportunity.

After a speaking engagement in Nashville, I had the night to myself, so I went to a nice steakhouse that overlooked the city. At first, I hesitated to go because I almost had to take out a loan just to pay for this dinner. Then I reminded myself, "Five-star place, five-star people. Suck it up Tori. Make it work." After the minuscule amount of convincing it took to take myself there, guess who I met that night. A billionaire. A billionaire who wanted his teenage daughter to go through my coaching programs. Another time while traveling to Vegas, I was so exhausted, all I wanted to do was order room service. But I knew that wouldn't be a wise use of my time. There were eleven thousand people at that hotel just for the personal development event I was attending—right there in the hotel—and I was thinking about hanging out in the room, not socializing, not connecting, just being in there by myself. I got my butt up, threw on my heels, freshened up my makeup, and did what I do best. I went to a steakhouse, sat at the bar, and ordered a nice dinner.

After a few minutes, the woman next to me sparked a conversation. She asked me what I did for a living, and I told her I owned a speaking and coaching business. She was intrigued. We shared a bit more about our lives, and I learned she and her husband owned a limo business and held an annual conference every year. Right then and there she asked me to speak on their stage.

Once while sitting in first class on a flight back home, I was next to a former pageant winner. She's now a very successful business owner in the real estate industry. We shared many stories about our lives on our three-hour flight home. Now when I look back on that plane ride, the thing I remember most was her genuine and humble heart. This successful woman had endured a lot of hardship through relationships, an experience that connected us. We laughed and cried together on that plane. Financially, we were on two different levels, but in that moment I realized, money doesn't bond you with other people; hearts do. While money is a reflection of what you've been able to accomplish, it isn't everything about you. It's so easy to look at what we perceive as someone's success and overlook what they've had to endure to get there. People with financial success have struggles and battles like everybody else.

I still keep in touch with my friend I bonded with on the plane that day, and I'll always remember the trust I felt as we told one another our stories. Being in the right place at the right time isn't always about what you can gain professionally. Sometimes, we meet the people we need on the journey of life who we can bless or who can bless us by helping each other through life's obstacles. The message you're sending as a walking billboard might be that you're joyful and can add that to someone's life, or that you're the angel they've needed to remind them that they're worthy and loved.

Tattoo this on your brain: you're one connection away from the life of your dreams. When you're actively showing up and moving in the same direction of your goals, you'll always be where you're supposed to be. Once you're there, be aware. Look for opportunities. They're all around you. Talk to that stranger. Listen to their stories.

Don't go into every place always ready to talk about yourself. Keep in mind that no matter how successful someone appears, they're still human. Also, pro tip: most successful people want to show you how to be successful, because they understand abundance multiplies and there's room for all of us at the table. Go to the steakhouse, buy the first-class ticket on a whim, spark conversation in the café, smile at the woman in the gym with killer abs. Show up every day, proud to be you. Your breakthrough is on the other side of hello.

. . . AND DOING SOMETHING MEMORABLE WHILE YOU'RE THERE

During my year as Miss Missouri USA, I had a chance to attend New York Fashion Week. As if that wasn't exciting enough, while I was in NYC, I also had an opportunity to visit the Miss Universe Organization (who owned Miss USA at the time). I was going to meet with the president and others who worked at the headquarters. However, I wanted to make sure they didn't forget about me as soon as I walked out the door. I had to leave my mark.

Knowing that most everybody in the world has a soft spot for sweets, I asked my coaches about the best bakery in the city. They pointed me in the direction of the place that made what they described as the best cupcakes in the world. Before I left Missouri for Fashion Week, I ordered the cupcakes. I also ordered customized cake flags with the 1st ManUp logo on them to stick in the cakes once I had them in hand. Once I got to New York, I picked up the cupcakes, stuck a flag into each one, and headed to the Miss Universe Headquarters.

The executives greeted me at the door and were thrilled about the unexpected yummy treats, their favorite cupcakes. I put them in the breakroom so when anyone who worked for the organization took some downtime that day, they'd open the box, grab a cupcake with a flag, and proceed to read the flyer I'd attached to the top of the box that explained who I was, what I stood for, and the 1st ManUp movement I'd created and intended to take to the Miss USA stage.

When you decide to do something, go ALL in. Think outside the box in everything that you do, dig into the corners of your creativity and do the things no one else is doing. Go the extra mile, shine your light, and leave an impression wherever you go. You never know who you'll meet, or who's hoping to meet you.

Chapter 11

FREE TO FAIL

It's about to get really real in this chapter. We're shifting gears, folks. You know there's times in our life when being real and vulnerable isn't always fun. Yep! This chapter is that moment for me. But you know what? I'm willing to dive in because I know you or someone you know may need to hear this. I didn't write this book for everyone to love me; I wrote this book to change lives by opening up and being bold. So buckle up; here goes nothin'.

My whole life, I've been a hopeless romantic. Hallmark Christmas channel? Count me in. Fa la la la Lifetime—heck yes! I'm a sucker for a good love story. I love love, and all my life, I've known I want to be married. I've never been one who dated just for the sake of dating. I always dated to see if there was a future. If not, I didn't make time for it. Because of that, I was eighteen years old when I had my first serious boyfriend. My family spent a lot of summers at the lake, and so did he. At first, our relationship was great. We enjoyed being together, and I genuinely liked him. He was safe, until the day he wasn't.

One day when we were together, things got heated. It kept going further and further. Because of my faith, I didn't have any intentions of establishing physical intimacy with him, but he had other ideas. I told him no, but he ignored it. He became forceful. I said no, then I said no again. Four noes later, all the respect he'd shown me up to that point had disappeared. Those moments took me down a path I'd never anticipated.

I was disgusted and felt completely violated. What in the world had just happened to me? How can a boyfriend rape you? Is that even possible? Lost and confused, I kept dating him long distance for a couple months after. I mean, it was my fault it had happened in the first place, right? I carried that belief around, putting all the blame on myself. Maybe I shouldn't have been alone with him; I'd put myself in that position. It took a long time to realize I'd been raped, and no, it wasn't my fault, and I needed to stop blaming myself, but that was only the beginning of breaking down the depths of the trauma that began that day.

When I was raped, my brain went through significant changes. From then on, I subconsciously believed that for a man to like me, I had to say yes to him all the time. I was nurturing unhealthy relationship patterns that would be harder to undo than they were to establish. The people-pleasing was in full force. While I was saying yes to men to make sure they were happy, I was saying no to myself, feeding a cycle of low self-esteem and powerlessness. I'd date a guy, hoping he was part of my future, while slowly pushing my own desires and values to the side. The more I did it, the more toxic things became.

Enter college. My first college boyfriend treated me great, and our relationship was fun and promising. One night after studying for finals, I dropped him off at his truck downtown. It was midnight, and I had to get up the next day for a math final that was going to either make or break my grade. I said goodnight, pulled out of the parking lot, and immediately noticed red and blue lights in my rearview mirror. I heard sirens. My phone rang.

"Hey," I answered.

"Hey, I'm going to jail," he responded. Who starts a conversation like that?!

"For what?"

"I'm going to jail, I can't talk, I gotta go."

Beep.

What the heck! We were just studying for finals, and now all of a sudden he's about to be locked up? My thoughts were racing. I had no clue what was going on. I was tired, confused, and in tears. I'd stopped my car, and when I looked back in the mirror, there he was, in handcuffs. Instead of spending the rest of the night resting up for my test, I was an emotional wreck, confused and questioning everything. Who was this guy, and what had he done to have the cops waiting to arrest him in the parking lot at midnight like that? He was so great, and I really liked him! How did I miss this? Of course, I told my parents who came through like champs. They reached out to their investigation team who found out that he had twenty-seven hits on his record. Twenty. Seven. Unraveling from that relationship was difficult. I broke things off, but after he was released, the harassment started. It was terrifying. Unfortunately, this wasn't the end of my dysfunctional relationships. I had done none of the necessary internal work to heal from my past hurts.

I was sitting in an airport one day when an entire baseball team floated down the escalator. I was single and thought a shower of gods was descending upon me. I got on the plane with two other passengers and an entire minor league baseball team. During the flight, one of them bought me a drink. We exchanged numbers, met up at one of his games, and had an instant connection. We were together for a while before he moved up a division in the minors and had to move from Iowa to California. No sweat, we'd just do the long-distance thing. Once we were no longer in the same city, things started to get questionable. What felt sure before had become iffy. I broke it off. Later, a friend came to visit me and decided to show me a new feature on social media that I wasn't aware of. When he pulled up the private unread messages I didn't know anything about, he found one from nine months prior that read, "Stop calling him your man and your boyfriend because he's married to my sister." It was my ex's sister-in-law. I was in utter shock. Betrayal doesn't even begin to describe it.

He owned up to the message, but he'd had me completely blindsided for almost a year. Things couldn't get any worse, right?

College carried on, and I met this man who I was sure was the love of my life. It was him, the man I was going to marry. Our upbringings seemed similar, and our personalities meshed. We had a blast every time we'd see each other downtown on the weekends or tailgating at the football games. But whenever I'd start to fall for him, he would back down, then I would back down and wait. I'd make excuses for him, like he wasn't ready yet, or it wasn't God's timing. We dated off and on, but I hoped we'd end up together. I knew we would.

Time passed and I graduated from college before him. I was moving into the next phase of life without him, but coincidentally we'd run into each other all over the country at random events. In my mind, seeing him so often was a reminder that we would be together when it was time, and I was right. The time came and we picked up where we'd left off . . . and then he left me to go back to his ex-girlfriend.

I'd had enough. No more games, no more back-and-forth. I was tired of feeling like an option and putting my hopes on someone who couldn't have cared less about me. I prepped to move to LA and pursue my new life in a new city and a new professional venture. I was totally focused on who I was becoming: a sports reporter and the next Miss Missouri USA. My mind was made up, until he came out to LA the first few weeks after I moved.

When we moved in together months later, I figured the rocky road we'd had was just the hard times we needed to prove our love to each other. Here comes happily ever after! Things were fine and dandy at the beginning. He seemed like everything I wanted, and he was saying everything I wanted to hear. The bliss only lasted a few weeks, however, he had expectations I didn't want to fulfill, but I had to make sure he was happy so I could hold on to the future I wanted us to have together. Every thought I had or action I took was for him. I didn't know it at the time, but my people-pleasing was turning into codependency. I thought I was being too harsh whenever I stood up for myself, I felt guilty if I told him no, and I excused a lack of emotional connection and understanding I never thought I'd tolerate, but I didn't know what this was or how to name it, and I certainly didn't know how to break away from it. On the outside, my life looked like a fairytale. Inside, I was drowning.

I won Miss Missouri USA and started my year with the crown. We were the ultimate power couple and had the day-to-day life to prove it—nice cars, boats, planes, a beautiful gated community—all of it. Everybody thought we were living the dream. Hashtag couple goals, right? I'd put on my crown and sash, walk into an appearance like a boss, greet people with smiles and hugs, then get in my car and fall apart. In the mornings during my time of gratitude and Scriptures, the time I'd spend to prepare mentally and spiritually for the day, I couldn't read without tears rolling down my face. I would make him breakfast as he was running out the door for work. As soon as he'd close the door, I'd burst into tears. I was on an emotional roller coaster. Issues started to come up that we hadn't discussed before moving in together.

When you enter into a serious relationship, would you please do me a favor first and make sure you and your significant other are aligned with your future goals? There is nothing more damaging to your career and relationship with a partner than being with someone who doesn't support your vision. You'll question yourself, and you might even allow them to talk you out of your dreams, then end up resenting them for it. Save yourself a lot of pain and ask the hard questions upfront. We butted heads about everything, and no matter how hard I tried, or how many counseling sessions we went to, nothing was going to change.

All the mindset work I'd done—the hours of training with coaches and mentors, practicing, creating opportunities for myself in the broadcasting space, convincing myself that I was worthy of my dreams and doing the work to get there—felt like it had all disappeared. When my confidence should have been at its highest, it was at its lowest. It was like I was in someone else's body watching them deconstruct into a broken mess.

When our relationship was crumbling, I visited a high school friend who was living in San Diego. She and I went out one night downtown, but I was extremely uncomfortable. I felt this strange fear because my boyfriend wasn't with me. I'd become timid and insecure in public without him there to protect me. When I zeroed in and noticed what I was feeling, I knew the problem was bigger than I'd previously thought. Awareness, no matter how big or small, is the first step to becoming a chain breaker of negative patterns if you're willing to listen to what your intuition is telling you.

You know by now that I go all in with everything I do. I give my all when I want something, including in my relationships. I was willing to do whatever it took to make this work with him. Finally, I spoke with a family member who helped me pinpoint what was happening to my self-confidence. I went straight to the bookstore and read obsessively for hours about different personality types and how they affect relationships. I didn't see my worth anymore. I was walking on eggshells. Every move I made depended on his decisions, but it wasn't until I realized this that I also realized I'd been doing this my whole life. I'd been people-pleasing in friendships, in business relationships, and in romantic relationships until I finally ended up losing Tori. I needed professional guidance. I knew I couldn't do this alone. I found an amazing counselor who ended up being a lifesaver.

In therapy, I learned a simple but profound lesson that would have saved me so much heartache: you can't change anybody. People change only if they want to. They are who they are, and it's up to us to believe that the behavior they're displaying right in front of our eyes is who they truly want to be. My therapist was one of the first teammates who helped repair my confidence. She helped me become aware of the manipulation and loss of self that was happening in my head, and ultimately, she helped me make an exit plan. I had one life, and I knew I didn't want to spend it like this.

Leaving was the hardest thing I'd ever done. He'd tried to convince me that I'd never been anything without him and I needed to stay. I moved out without him knowing because I was afraid I wouldn't have the strength to leave if he was there. Pulling out of that driveway shattered me to pieces. With my mom in the front seat and the city in the rearview mirror, I said goodbye to my past. Once I'd removed all my belongings, I traveled down to where he was so I could officially end things in person. It was an unbearable pain. That wasn't the end, though. A friend's wedding was coming up.

I knew that if I went to this wedding, I would crumble and go back to him, so I called my friend to tell her I loved her but had to put myself first this time. I'd never said this to a friend before. I just prayed she would understand. She thought I was being selfish, but I had to protect my heart. I knew I couldn't put myself in a vulnerable situation. Canceling on her was gut-wrenching for me and deal-breaking for her. I lost many close friends because of that one decision my future self will always thank me for.

It took years to recover from that breakup. Being with him was like a drug; it just kept calling me back until either I was ready to walk away or it destroyed me. It was my difficult choice to leave, and it was the hardest thing I've ever done, but it changed the trajectory of my life. There were signs along the way. Once, after we kissed, I told him I loved him for the first time. In what was a moment of vulnerability for me, he burped in my face. Red flags, don't ignore them. Giving things my all is a blessing and a curse. That time, it backfired, but because I left, God opened so many more doors for me personally and romantically. Finally allowing myself to "give up" saved me. Now I can give gratitude for that experience because it led me to the most incredible relationship of my life.

Three months after I said goodbye, I presented my biggest keynote up to that point in front of two thousand people. Every time I've gone through hardship or had a major breakthrough, my mentors and coaches have been there to hold me accountable to my goals. This time, those godsends were my speaking coach, my therapist, and of course, my fam.

Looking back, I can trace all those dysfunctional relationships back to when I was raped. Since I hadn't done the internal work to heal, I was attracting unhealthy relationships. We attract who we are. I'd been taught all my life to be strong and stand up for myself, but trauma interrupted that conditioning and started a cycle that led me to the lowest point in my life. I honestly believe that had I not experienced what I did at the age of eighteen, I wouldn't have gone through all the subsequent brokenness. If you see destructive patterns in your own behavior, pinpoint where they come from and dig until you find the root. Give yourself grace through that process. Once I uncovered these truths within myself, I felt a sense of freedom and acceptance, a pleasant change from codependency.

Sometimes, situations unwillingly force you to recognize your weaknesses and rebuild on a firm foundation. I unexpectedly learned things about myself that I'll carry with me forever. One of those lessons was how to establish and enforce boundaries. Boundaries are vital for your happiness, self-confidence, and health in relationships. Without them, there are people out there who will always push you past your limits for their own advantage. You are the only one who can stop this.

It's a mistake to think strong, independent women don't get caught up in these kinds of situations. It happens more than you think. Just because someone's life looks ideal on the outside doesn't mean it's all butterflies and rainbows behind closed doors. Never assume anyone has it perfect, and always remember you have the power to change your life. Always.

Chapter 12

UNLOCKING INTERNAL BREAKTHROUGH

When you finally find yourself on the other side of adversity, in a place where you can see things for what they are with eyes of acceptance and forgiveness, you can start to make adjustments. The rawness hangs around for a while as a reminder of the road you don't want to turn down again. I'd made a pivotal decision for my life to take a stand and put a stop to this unhealthy relationship cycle. Although it was far from easy, it would mean an overhaul to my deepest core beliefs, patterns, and thought processes. I was up for the challenge. The one thing I've always wanted is a healthy romantic relationship with a man who has a heart to serve, loves Jesus, is compassionate, loving, respectful, and loves to have fun! But I realized before you can have what you want, you first have to be ready to attract and receive it into your life. I stood there, facing all the vulnerable truths about my past and realizing the behaviors had started small and grown into powerhouses. I had to lose myself to find myself.

In my case, it started with my surroundings. I needed to move away from the environment that was not serving my bigger vision for my future. I wasn't my best self in the surroundings I was in, and since I was in control of my living situation, I removed myself from a place that was mentally tearing me down and settled somewhere else that would lift me higher: hello, Scottsdale, Arizona!

A fresh start is exciting, but starting over takes a lot of work. I had to make all new friends, figure out how to build my business, and restore a Tori who was eager to find the best version of herself. I vowed to myself that I would never again settle for anything but my happiest life. I threw away all of the limiting beliefs about how old I'd be when I found my better half or a timeline for my professional achievements. My new priorities were simple: I wanted to be genuinely happy again and mentally healthy. That was all. My next step was to fully grieve the loss of leaving a man I cared so deeply about. I had to grieve the dreams I'd attached to us being together, and I had to grieve the loss of the person I hoped he was going to become and the life we were building. Grief isn't just for death. Your best choices can sometimes be the most heartbreaking, but just know, God is with you every step of the way. Most of the time, to unlock your future, you have to go through pain and brokenness first. It's a rite of passage that sets you up to truly appreciate happiness once you've found it.

I was on the journey to do the work. I discovered my trigger points, what made me happy, sad, joyful, angry, moody, emotional—all the things. It was exhausting, profound internal work that honestly, most people aren't willing to face. It takes too much time and effort, and hey, it's not me, it's them, right? Not at all. If you keep finding yourself in hurtful situations, consider the common denominator. It doesn't make you a bad person, but it might mean you have some root work to do, and once you do it, you'll know freedom in a way you haven't before. I was able to push through the healing process because I was sure God would prevail over any disaster or heartbreak.

As I examined my life and took ownership for my circumstances, I got to know myself on new levels that created breakthroughs in my life. I became aware of how I showed up in all kinds of relationships and situations and realized that, shoot, I guess I wasn't perfect after all! Some patterns are naturally passed on through generations and others have been created on your own. One of my biggest motivators is the thought of having children one day and never wanting them to have to go through the pains I did because I didn't take the time to heal from them. Of course, they will have their own "stuff" to work through and make their own mistakes, but by staying up on my personal development and awareness of generational patterns, I can only hope that I am also paving the way for my kids.

There's a natural pressure from the outside world that can influence how we feel about ourselves on the inside if we haven't done the internal examination. We as humans place tremendous worth on the elements people see on the outside.

I was so concerned with what others thought of me that I'd forgotten what I thought about myself. I needed to remember who I was, so I dove headfirst into literature about boundaries and healing: Joyce Meyers' *Healing the Soul of a Woman*; *Psychopath Free and Whole Again* by Jackson MacKenzie; and my favorite, *You Are a Badass* by Jen Sincero. These books changed my world. They shifted my perspective and filled the empty places of my heart that I didn't even know needed attention. Those books were a microscope for my heart and soul. Not only did I unlock areas of my life that had been sealed for so long, I gained tools to win the struggle in my mind.

I realized that without pain, there's no power. The real power comes from what you do with your pain. It's up to you to either make it a prison or construct your God-given purpose out of it. The bricks I used to build my purpose were forgiveness of myself and those who'd hurt me, thankfulness for the circumstances that shaped me, and focus on the beauty in the struggle.

I had to completely and freely grieve my past to welcome my best future. I had to be okay with the idea of failing in my relationship to finally start a new chapter. That freedom to fail, to get to the point where I knew I'd given my all and couldn't give anything else, opened the door for me to give up. Soon after, I realized I hadn't failed at all. Instead, I got on the road to freedom and happiness. Since I'm a coach and I love action steps, I can't just tell you all this without giving you practical actions for how to do it yourself. Techniques give you the reassurance that you can reach the level of happiness you're striving for. Here's what I did to overcome the trauma and find myself again:

- Prayed like my life depended on it
- Hugged my momma
- Set my pride and ego aside and let family and friends help me
- Researched PTSD and emotional trauma therapists who introduced me to Eye Movement Desensitization and Reprocessing (EMDR) therapy
- Talked to counselors and told them my story so I could remove it from my mind and body
- Wrote a letter to myself and journaled my thoughts and feelings
- Read multiple self-help books to rewire my thinking

- Cried every second I could, endured the painful nights, and let my heart feel the hurt
- Removed people from my life who weren't supportive
- Avoided areas in my life that triggered me
- Surrounded myself with Christians and people I wanted to be more like
- Attended a church that resonated with me
- Leaned on my support system
- Started to date myself. I wrote fifty date ideas on fifty wooden sticks and put them in a jar. Every week, I'd draw a stick and take myself on a date, even if I didn't want to.
- Listened to my intuition
- Made a conscious decision to focus on my business
- Stayed dedicated to my routine
- Created my dream environment at home
- Focused on everything I DID want in a relationship instead of what I didn't want
- Didn't give up on myself

Once you've been through some of the most trying times, you become clear on what you will and won't tolerate. Do the work to learn those things, then hang on to them. Don't settle. You only get one life. You have to decide for yourself how you're going to live it.

Chapter 13

SO YOU WANT TO BE AN ENTREPRENEUR?

I'm proud of myself for the way I woke up one morning and was magically successful. I'm proud of everyone else who opened their eyes one day and had achieved all the goals they'd written down the day before but hadn't worked for. It sounds ridiculous because it is—success never happens like that! As much as it makes for good TV and we want to believe we can stumble on a life-changing win one day, nobody is an overnight success.

It's funny when people make that assumption because nothing could be further from the truth. The entire time I competed in pageants, I was strategically planning to live out my purpose when the lights went out on the stage for me for the last time. Even if I won Miss USA, I knew pageantry couldn't last forever. I'd probably live many more decades after that last competition, so I'd better be planning for life after as much as I was preparing for interviews and catwalks. Miss USA was never meant to be an end-all-be-all.

I remember standing on the Miss USA stage waiting to see who the fifteenth and final semifinalist would be. They called the name, and it wasn't mine. That was the end of the road for me in pageantry, but it was just the beginning of my professional endeavors. My parents were sitting in the front row, and when the announcer didn't call my name, I looked at them and said, "God has a plan." I was hurt because I had mentally prepared to go much further in the competition, all the way to the crown. I didn't know exactly what my next step would be, but I did know there was something else awesome in store for me. Sometimes, when an opportunity doesn't pan out like we hoped, we're being prepared for something more designed for us and protected from something else. I felt the necessary feelings, cried, and ate some chocolate covered peanuts the second I got off stage. Soon after the competition, I rested in the fact that all the networking, speaking, strategizing, and creating I'd done in the years leading up to this moment would pay off and make everything worthwhile. All the seeds I'd planted were going to come to fruition.

I went home after the pageant and sat at the kitchen counter with Trav. I'd spent so much time crafting my purpose. I knew I wanted to be a motivational speaker, but I was done with pursuing sports reporting. The entrepreneur in me was screaming to be set free. I'd done the work to build my platform. On top of that, I'd been through the wringer in pageantry, losing five times before getting to my win. I had a story to tell.

"What do I do now?" I asked my brother.

In his matter of fact, black-and-white, coach-like manner, he said, "You've been a loser more than you've been a winner. You need to help the losers."

"Well isn't that the truth!" We laughed, and I agreed.

In the mind of an athlete, you either win or you lose. There are many, many more girls who lose pageants than those who win, more athletes who lose than win, more politicians who lose than win. Everybody might get a trophy, but not everybody gets a title. Losing is a common experience, but no matter how much we experience it, it never gets easier. When you don't walk away with the gold, it's hard. It messes with your head and makes you doubt your hard work and what you thought you knew. I knew people needed to learn to lose with their self-worth intact instead of losing their identity in the process, so I created a coaching structure around my knowledge and experiences.

Trav and I sat there and planned the basics of the seven-week program I'd craft. We made a rough draft of what the coaching service would look like. I meditated on my competition journey, everything I'd been through, how I persevered through it, how I took every no like a boxer takes a shot to the stomach and kept pressing on toward my yes, and how I kept my grit and maintained my confidence enough to keep going.

Six attempts at something are a lot, so most people give up before it gets to that point. I'd put in an uncountable amount of hours of training year after year, so Trav and I brainstormed the formula of practical steps and the order of events I took every time I lost. We thought it through, planned it out, and made it happen—we made it happen like amateurs, but we did it.

Getting started was a comedy of errors. I didn't know how to film on my computer. I ended up using the wrong type of camera and stumbled through the most basic editing software after my brother spent a day teaching me the basics. More than once, when I was interviewing a special guest, I filmed a video to post online and forgot to press record, so the guest had to come back a second time to record again. I didn't know what would work or where to start, so I just started where I was and made so many mistakes. But honestly, if you wait until you have all the knowledge and everything is perfect, you'll never take the first step. My only requirement was that I wouldn't do anything that anybody else was already doing. I wanted uniqueness to be my calling card. If that meant grinding and struggling daily to figure out something new, so be it. Some of those ideas came after sleepless nights, others came after restful nights, but none of my success came overnight.

I was finding my footing with my coaching venture and ended up training quite a few girls on mindset and confidence, but when I really thought about it, I felt like a hypocrite. During my first year of business, I was still in the relationship that had taken a major toll on my confidence. It was a mental tug-of-war. Although I had years of experience, I was coaching my clients on something I needed to work on myself at the time. When I took them through modules or calls, I was talking to me just as much as I was talking to them about what they needed to do. My confidence was on life support. I gave them my best, and thankfully they got great results, but I suddenly felt like I was not being an authentic leader. So what did I do about it? I got the help I needed and realized that nobody has ever "arrived." As long as I didn't stay stagnant, I wasn't a hypocrite at all. I had many techniques to share from my years of experience, but I couldn't coach myself. This was only one of the places where I was doing the work behind closed doors that other people didn't see, which I learned is a staple of entrepreneurship.

When you first launch a business or start anything new, for that matter, people are excited. "You're killing it! You're crushing it!" they say. When I moved to Los Angeles to pursue modeling and reporting, I got messages from a couple of friends raving about fame and asking what movie I was going to be in. The novelty of starting over is fun and exciting, but the moment-to-moment is scary and can get pretty lonely at times. Expectations don't line up with reality most of the time, and what you see of someone on the outside may very well not line up with what they're going through in their private lives. I was crushing it, right? Sure, if you call having a one-person staff meeting every two hours in my mirror to keep my confidence at a workable level "crushing it."

As a new entrepreneur, I didn't understand finances. I was terrible at budgeting personal and business life. This is just another one of those things people think they can judge without knowing what's happening under the surface. They saw the flowers, but they didn't see the planting process. When people pay for your product or service, they aren't paying for an hour of your time on a video call; they are paying for the years of work, time, and investments in coaches and mentors that you've hired for yourself to reach the level of expertise they're benefitting from.

From the start, I was fortunate to have a practical coaching program and speaking opportunities other people would have fought me on the street for, but I wasn't making a fortune from them because I hadn't yet tapped into the power of exposure as the new kid on the block. After a crazy amount of time, trial and error, repetition, evaluation, and re-evaluation, I finally realized how I could help women enhance their lives and value myself appropriately. Even after you think you've nailed it, it's not a one-and-done kind of thing. Entrepreneurship is a continuous process of discovery, creativity, overcoming, practicing, understanding, overdelivering, and creating excellent content so people see real change in their lives because of it.

It goes without saying that clients are the lifeblood of a business. When you first start out in business, you have a picture in your head of the ideal client who you think will end up being a forever client. I put a great deal of energy into nailing down who those clients would be for me, and now those people aren't even my niche anymore. Your first clue about who's not the ideal client? Someone! Who! Doesn't! Pay! I know it sounds crazy, but it's more common than you think.

Look, you're either running a business or a charity. Early on, I was running a charity and calling it a business. You have to be willing to really put yourself out there, take guidance from God and other successful people in your space, and stay persistent. When you let your passion drive you, the money will come. I started my business in 2018. It was really starting to grow when the pandemic hit in 2020, which I consider my real first full year of business. While the world was shutting down, I buckled down. I interviewed the highest caliber influencers for my podcast up to that point, created my signature keynote, and launched my new coaching programs. Nothing could stop me from pushing forward. That year was a difficult year for the world. Things were falling apart and breaking all around us. Sadness blanketed country after country. Many people didn't have a choice in what happened to them that year professionally, but since I was one of the fortunate ones who did, I chose to push forward as hard as I could, which set the stage for the next year.

In 2021, I practiced my butt off to land some of the biggest speaking engagements I'd had yet. I would write and rewrite my speeches throughout the nights, practice my keynote in front of the camera, and focus on my fitness and nutrition right when it would have been easier to order pizza and sit on the couch. I needed to be the best leader I could be so I could be at my best for the people I wanted to serve.

Going into 2022, year four, I knew where I wanted to go, I just needed to pause and tweak the plan to see what was working to get me there and what wasn't. I gave myself permission to reconstruct. I restructured whatever wasn't serving my clients at the highest possible capacity and gave myself permission to do something totally unexpected. You know what I did? I canceled coaching clients. I know—it sounds so crazy! But I knew God was calling me to redirect my efforts to make space for the doors that would soon open. When I did that, God showed up and showed off with blessings in my life, some expected, some not.

Four years in, and I'm just getting started, but you and I both know this journey has been much longer than the four years since I formed my official corporation. My pageant journey was full of failing, getting back up, analyzing, and trying again. I had to learn to become what I wanted instead of just working toward it. These ventures become my passion, not just a way to spend the time. To get better, I focused on learning from the best and practicing what I preach.

When it comes to your life, it's okay to pivot and reflect, or even restart. The freedom is yours to curate your life the way you want. If something shifts—your plans, circumstances, or even your mindset—realign and set a new track. It's okay to stop doing what isn't serving your people or yourself. When someone looks at you showing up, stepping out, and leveling up and assumes they know what you did to get there, let them. Keep in mind for yourself that nothing substantial can be built overnight. The next time someone calls you an overnight success, just smile, wink, and keep doing your thang.

Chapter 14

THE SECRET BEHIND EVERY DREAM

From time to time, you learn something that changes the game in ways you couldn't have imagined. Visualization and manifestation were those things for me. I was just like most people who hear these ideas for the first time, thinking they were new age woo-woo, but it wasn't long before I opened my mind and tried it for myself.

It's about the Law of Attraction: what you think of and talk about consistently is what you will attract into your life. When I aligned my thoughts and actions with my true desires and started placing myself in the right environments, it was insane how the things I wanted began to show up in my life. It's been about a decade since my first encounter with this concept, and things haven't been the same since.

It all started when I went to Arkansas to train with my runway coach, Kim, and saw her Mercedes SUV parked in her garage.

"I love your car," I said.

"Oh, thanks! I totally manifested that," she replied.

"Totally manifested that? What do you mean?"

"I manifested my car, my husband—all the things I've dreamed about having." Kim said.

At first, I was a bit baffled, but I was also intrigued by the thought that I could manifest a car and a husband.

She explained how she had written down the traits she wanted in a partner, visualized a man who had all those traits, and prayed about it. Sure enough, years later, she had her dream man and dream family. Of course I could have doubted her and blown the whole thing off, but looking at the blessings in her life that backed up her claims, I knew I had to learn more.

People who are winning in life are almost always willing to share their methods with you. What makes all the difference is whether you're willing to listen or not. Angelina Lombardo, author of *A Spiritual Entrepreneur*, writes, "manifesting is making everything you want to feel and experience a reality, via your thoughts, actions, beliefs, and emotions[5]."

This was a new concept for me, but instead of pushing against it (especially since I trusted the person who was telling me about it) I opened my ears and mind as she explained the process of seeing a desire in your mind's eye, praying about it, and then intentionally making moves in your life to welcome it in, all with gratitude. Next, my coach recommended I read *The Secret*, which I did as soon as I got home.

---

5   https://www.oprahdaily.com/life/a30244004/how-to-manifest-anything/

The Secret introduced me to the concept of a vision board, a visible reminder of all your dreams, goals, and desires. I bought a board and printed pictures of all the things I wanted in every area of my life: my health, family, relationships, finances, house, charities, foundations, my future family complete with my dream man, a yacht, a private plane, my dream SUV, a motorhome to trek across the nation with my future fam—everything I could think of went on that board. Complete with photos and quotes I live by, it became the snapshot of every desire that had been spinning inside my head. My board hangs in my room where I'm naturally seeing it several times a day.

For years, I've wanted to build personal development and sports facilities in impoverished countries to teach children life skills and show them immense love and possibilities. As a motivational speaker, one of my goals is to fill stadiums across the nation (and eventually, the world) with thousands of people to connect with others, learn more about themselves, and level up in their lives. I want to own a beach house somewhere that feels like paradise. I want to maintain my ideal health. There are several Bible verses close to my heart that keep my faith at the forefront of my mind. All of these things are posted on my vision board.

One of my favorite things about the dream board is that you take things off as you achieve them. So far, I've been able to take off competing for Miss USA, starting my own business, creating an online course, launching a podcast, and writing a book. Wish me luck, because this will be a big organizational undertaking for me, but the goal is to one day make a scrapbook of all the things I've taken off the board as a reminder of how far I've come. When there are too many gaps on the board, I challenge myself to dream bigger and more outside the box. I take my time filling in the spaces with new photos and imagining myself achieving every single thing, which motivates me to make the sacrifices to make my dreams come true.

One element of visualization and manifestation is connecting your emotions to the outcome. I have a picture of my future husband and me dancing at our wedding. When I look at that picture, I imagine all of the emotions that I'll have when that moment is happening in real time: how happy I'll be, who will be there, what music will be playing, who will be obnoxiously banging their wine glass with a fork to get us to kiss. I think of all the exhilaration I'll feel when I put myself inside the reality of my goals and dreams.

When I had winning Miss Missouri USA on the board, along with a picture of a crown and sash, I made visualizing that goal part of my morning routine. I would read Scripture, sit in silence, meditate, and feel the crown being placed on my head and the sash being draped on my shoulder. I felt my hands clasping the hands of the other final contestant (with my hands on top, because that's what you're supposed to do when you're expecting to win a pageant). I imagined the emcee calling my name and exactly how they'd say it. I saw myself crying, pointing up toward God, seeing my parents and brother crying in the audience while the rest of my family and friends went wild, and hearing the sound of the audience cheering for my crowning moment. By the time I'd won, I'd already been there in my heart and mind.

Manifestation holds so much power, and it's available to all of us. If you can see your dream behind your eyes, you can create it in your life. Make it a daily habit to visualize your dreams and attach your emotions to how you'll feel once they are reality. Then, while you're doing the work, the rewards will start coming to you. Still skeptical? Read what Psychology Today has to say about it:

Brain studies now reveal that thoughts produce the same mental instructions as actions. Mental imagery impacts many cognitive processes in the brain: motor control, attention, perception, planning, and memory. So the brain is getting trained for actual performance during visualization. It's been found that mental practices can enhance motivation, increase confidence and self-efficacy, improve motor performance, prime your brain for success, and increase states of flow—all relevant to achieve your best life[6]!

Our minds hold the key to the change we want to see in our lives. You have the power and access to get inside of your dream as if it's happening right now in your life, feel it in the core of your being, and set things into motion. To make sure my life aligns with the desires of my heart, I strategically place reminders all around me to align my senses with my future reality. There are pictures all around my home of palm trees, beaches, and colorful sunsets. I'm careful about the music I listen to and the movies I watch because I don't want negativity in my head. I'm obsessed with motivational coffee mugs; I could never have too many. Since they're one of the first things I see every morning, I make sure they're covered in reminders of my dreams. On two occasions, I visited the gift shops of TV shows I'd like to appear on in New York City, and I bought mugs with those shows' names on them. I desire a husband, so I have a mug that says "hubby" on it and sometimes fill it with coffee when I fill my own cup, because one morning, I'll wake up, have coffee with my husband, and read devotions with him to start off my day. This small action, which might seem kind of crazy to some, sends the message to the Universe that I'm ready for this moment in my life. I have mugs that say "Goal Getter," some with Bible verses on them, and others with places I'd like to live one day. If you see my

6   https://www.psychologytoday.com/us/blog/flourish/200912/
        seeing-is-believing-the-power-visualization

home, you'll never question who I'm becoming, because pieces of the future me are everywhere.

When you start to rewire your brain for manifestation, you'll find yourself needing to undo some limiting beliefs from your past. One of the most common areas for limiting beliefs is money. We want it, but we feel like we're not supposed to want it. Forget that. Money is great. It provides access and opportunities for you and for others, and who doesn't want that? To bring more money into my life, I leave it sitting around my house in places where I'll see it. I want to send the message out to the Universe that since money is available and everywhere, it's flowing into my life. Shifting my attitude toward money has required letting go of limiting beliefs around it. The more I see it, the more it becomes part of my life instead of something distant or difficult to acquire. The kicker is, once you have the money, are you being a good steward of it? Are you honoring it, using it for your life's needs, and staying faithful in tithing and helping those in need? I'm a firm believer that God will bless you with more finances when he sees that you are using it for good, which then will attract more money into your life. The same goes for everything else on my vision board. I have motivational quotes hanging up behind my desk, like, "Winners aren't people who never fail, but people who never quit," and "Live your dream." You can do this in whatever format works for you, but just make sure you do it! Take time to think about what you want, write it down, print it out, and post your dreams around your house. Doing this brings them one step closer to reality.

Let's be real—as women, we spend a lot of time in front of the bathroom mirror. Another way to train your mind to believe in the person you're becoming is to write affirmations on your mirror. You can write directly on your mirror with a dry-erase marker, or you can do what I do, which is write affirmations on sticky notes and post those on the mirror. Either way, here are some of my favorites:

- Humility never goes out of style.

- God created me to stand out, not fit in.

- Tell someone how much they're loved today.

- I am unapologetically Tori.

- I choose to be happy in this present moment.

- Be who you want to be, not who the world tells you to be.

- My body is strong and healthy.

- I am living the life of my dreams today.

I change up my bathroom mirror affirmations depending on what I am currently facing in that season of life, need to attract more of, or am ready to manifest, including becoming an author. In my living room, I have the books that have helped me along my personal development journey. My books sit behind the clear door of my console table so I can see them, which helped me manifest writing my first book. Most of them are self-help, my favorite genre. The three decorative books on my coffee table include the words motivation, mindfulness, and success. I have carefully curated my home as a place that will uplift me, surround me with positivity, encourage me, and keep me in a place of wholeness. Because I've designed my environment in this way, these mantras are my default. Due to my surroundings, I am manifesting my life in the present moment for the future. I encourage you to create an environment in your own home that supports and uplifts you, too.

You can't just hope for things and expect them to come to you. Dream, pray, manifest, take action. Repeat. This new intentional routine will be a source of joy. You have the power to create whatever you want, so make it fun, exciting, and encouraging. Your future self will thank you for it!

Chapter 15

OWN YOUR IDENTITY

When you're a kid, everybody asks what you want to be when you grow up. More than likely, you're answering based upon something that your parents or someone in your sphere of influence is doing for their career. You choose a college or form of ongoing education based on what can equip you for the work you'll do day in and day out. When you meet new people, after they ask your name (which they often forget five seconds later), they ask what you do for a living. When you retire, you tell people what you did all those years before and what you plan to do with all your new free time. How many times have you ever introduced yourself to someone and had them ask, after they forgot your name, "Who are you?" Probably zero.

We have a hard time detaching who we are from what we've accomplished. We find our worth in the list of achievements we can rattle off on a resume, and when someone else's list is longer or more impressive, we ask ourselves, "What am I even doing?" This was an unhealthy cycle for me until I discovered who I was.

I've been religious my whole life, but I didn't have a real relationship with Jesus until I found the Mosaic Church in Hollywood, California in 2017. I was Lutheran growing up, so my faith had a strong foundation, but when I went to Mosaic, for the first time, I felt the presence of God on a whole new level. I felt the Holy Spirit moving through me like I was fully known, understood, forgiven, and heard. This did more for my confidence and fully discovering who I was than anything else. That sense of knowing gave me a strong foundation to build my self-worth on.

As a high achiever, I'd gotten used to attaching a lot of my self-worth to my performance, as if I was worth more when I was performing at my best. Only recently have I realized I don't have to be the best to be accepted by God or the people who love me. I am Tori, and that is enough.

This journey of self-discovery is one heck of a trip. It requires you to peel back the layers of what makes you, you—the hurtful things, the experiences you'd rather forget, what makes you happy, and everything in between. It's digging into your upbringing, wins, and losses with rawness and truth and asking, "How have I defined my worth?" When I was younger, my worth was based on how I performed in basketball. After that, it was the leadership positions I held in different organizations in college. Anytime I could check off another achievement, I felt like I'd "made it," like I'd proven something important to myself and anybody else who was paying attention. When I didn't win, I doubted everything. This is all due to my performance-based personality.

Don't get me wrong; a lot of great things can come from a performance-based personality, like audacious goals, a killer work ethic, and the ability to make smart adjustments. But man, it also can take a toll on your mind if your identity gets wrapped up in it all. Once I realized I was loved and accepted for who I was, not what I was, I was able to show up as ME in the world. There was no need or space for me to walk around in a fake identity. That serves no one. I had to take ownership of who God created me to be in this world: the outgoing, fun, bubbly, strong, opinionated, authentic, high-achieving woman. No matter if the atmosphere is positive or negative, remember you always have a choice to change it. Don't dim your light to make others feel comfortable. As with anything else, staying in this positive headspace is constant, daily work, but it's worth it to reach personal freedom. While it is necessary to recognize, embrace, and celebrate your successes, placing your worth on those things can be self-destructive.

If you've been living in the performance-based mindset for a period of time, it can be hard to figure out how to undo those beliefs and create new patterns of thinking. I went through the process with journaling and reading books that all helped me discover my identity beyond the court, stage, and leadership positions. I took the time to go through exercises like writing down my core personal values, my life mission, what makes me, me, my strengths, and talents—everything that had nothing to do with a specific outcome but made me who I am. God made each of us unique for a reason, and no two are the same. Embrace your one-of-a-kind identity.

One of the most trying journeys of self-discovery for me was after I'd detached myself from unhealthy relationships. Once that part of the process was done, I had to regroup, find myself again, and figure out what kind of life I wanted to build.

When it comes to self-discovery, it all comes down to having the guts to be real and raw with yourself. If you can't be honest about what you love about yourself and where you can improve, then you can't make adjustments. If you can't make adjustments, you can't grow. You can't serve the people around you at the highest capacity. Instead of your life being in alignment, you become stagnant, and you and I both know that no one thrives while being complacent.

If you're looking for a way to unleash your highest self, try sitting down and writing out your thoughts and visions. Write down what you want for your life. Make that vision board. Put up posters of the things you desire to have and places you want to go. Assemble your dreams on a board that you will see every day in every area of your life to remind you of why you do what you do. Create your dream and step into it fully.

In a college classroom, an English professor asked his class who they were. He said, "If you take away all the organizations, teams, grades, accolades, what dorm or apartment complex you live in, what cars you drive, what would be left?" The class was silent. Nobody really knew how to answer the question.

If you're a nurse by trade, or a lawyer, a doctor, or an engineer, that's your working title, but that's not who you are. I was at a speaking engagement once, and the host asked the members of the panel to introduce ourselves. A couple of the speakers answered, "I'm an author," "I'm a coach," or rattled off statistics about all the stuff they'd sold or how many years they'd been doing something most anybody would find impressive. For a long time, I would introduce myself by saying, "I'm Miss Missouri USA 2018, and I'm passionate about helping women create the life of their dreams." Recently, one of my speaking mentors showed me a new way to introduce myself. Now I say, "I'm Tori Kruse, and it's a pleasure to be here with you today. Before I tell you what I do, I want you to know who I am. I'm a strong believer. I'm a daughter, sister, and loyal friend. And I'm on a mission to help women become everything they're meant to be. What do I do? I'm a speaker, coach, author, and Miss Missouri USA 2018."

If you're on a stage, people know you've probably done something to earn that spot. But what people can relate to more than your achievements is the genuineness of who you are as a person. Stop with the phoniness, people. No one likes a fake. I challenge you to start introducing yourself this way and just see how people's body language and responses change toward you. It's also a great filter to weed out the people you don't want to work with. If they only want to be around you because of your achievements, that means they want to try to somehow capitalize on it. I never want someone to want to work with me for those reasons. I want them to see my heart, passion, and fierce tenacity to succeed, and then have our energies match up. That's when great things happen.

I had a friend who would only introduce me to people as Miss Missouri USA; it was like she'd forgotten my name. I was proud of my accomplishment, and I was happy that she was proud of it too, but it made me feel like our friendship was solely based upon my crown and sash. It got to the point where I would roll my eyes, chuckle, and reintroduce myself on my own, "Hi, my name is Tori. Nice to meet you. And yes, I am also Miss Missouri," as I would sigh slightly under my breath. I never wanted to be defined by my crown. I want people to see me for who I am first, not what I've accomplished. This kind of introduction seemed to be going against everything that I believed in, especially as a first impression.

One of my greatest missions and challenges during my reign as Miss Missouri USA was not allowing my full identity to get wrapped up in my title. I wasn't always successful, but I was always mindful of it and did the work to stay focused. I was proud and happy to be in that position, but I knew I had a life outside of pageantry and a career that would span far beyond the year of my life after winning the title. In fact, one of the reasons I wasn't devastated after not winning Miss USA is because I focused on discovering my God-given purpose through the journey with the future in sight, not just pageantry. And it saved me big time. My goal was to leverage the crown to benefit others and my own future, so I was always thinking ahead. Throughout the year, when I went somewhere to serve or speak, I'd look at it as a way to create my own speaking business and take the lessons I was learning so I could pass them on to somebody else later. I've created a course to help pageant girls develop their purpose through the journey instead of waiting until after the journey is over, because that's when the downward spiral comes in and you lose your identity. While living in the present moment is good, when you're in a position where you know your time is limited, you have to be forward thinking so you don't lose yourself in the process. Even if you do win and advance to the next level, at some point you're still going to have to change your path. Always be thinking about how your present is impacting your future, and always be ready to adjust your mindset based on the goal at hand.

Positive thoughts bring positive results, while negative thoughts bring negative results. I had to mentally become Miss USA before I ever competed for Miss Missouri USA. In high school, I had to believe I was the best 3-point shooter before I could become the leading 3-point shooter. I need to believe I'm the world's greatest motivational speaker before I actually am. This might make you feel like a fraud, like you're faking it until you make it. It might make you feel like you're not worthy of these accomplishments and you don't have what it takes, no matter what others see in you or even the skills you've developed to that point. Don't let those limiting beliefs stop you.

When my confidence feels shaken, I take a step back and reframe what's happening. I see it for the internal conflict it is, and I refuse to let the enemy steal, kill, or destroy what I know I'm meant to do. When this happens, I remind myself that I'm right where I'm supposed to be.

Throughout my twenties and even still today, there are times when my insecurities pop up like an annoying fly that won't stop buzzing around my head. At one point in my pageant journey, I was convinced I had to own a Louis Vuitton bag to place at Miss USA. That is a bunch of bull honky if I've heard it. Although, I can't lie, I am a bit boujee, and I do like a good Louis Vuitton bag, but that does not mean I needed one to win the dang pageant. However, looking through social media told me otherwise. I always put pressure on myself to look put-together, and it wasn't cool or comfortable to expose my vulnerabilities. The year I won, I was going through some of the darkest times of my personal life. Now that I've gone through the process and done the internal work of uprooting what made me insecure, I'm much more comfortable sharing the parts of me that make me most human. I was "publicly judged" for many years, and now it feels good to break free from the opinion of others. Now, I openly share my insecurities and fears, not to have a pity party, but because when I'm vulnerable with my struggles it provides a space to let others open up as well.

The journey to self-belief can be especially difficult if we don't give ourselves permission to explore our thoughts, likes, and potential apart from what other people have told us our whole lives. It wasn't until I moved away from my hometown that I was able to start relying on my own inner voice in addition to, and sometimes instead of, the voices that had guided me my whole life. When I left home, I started to discover and create my own identity. New environments lead to new experiences and new people, all of which mold you into the person you're meant to become. When you're away from what you've always known, you start to rely on your intuition more. I call that voice inside of me the Holy Spirit. Whether you call it the Holy Spirit, intuition, little voice, or something else, when you pay attention to it, you'll find your path to freedom and unleash your most powerful self.

From the time we're born, we're conditioned to listen to our parents. It totally makes sense. They feed us, keep us safe, and teach us the basics of life. Plus, if you don't listen, you may just get in trouble. As a kid, listening to your parents all the time isn't always your top priority. But then comes freedom. You grow up. You have choices other than what kind of cereal you'll eat for breakfast or what you want somebody to get you for Christmas. Hopefully, you begin to listen to and trust yourself. Of course you'll screw up, make bad decisions, and question your life choices sometimes, but other times, you'll try new things, surprise yourself with brilliance you didn't know you had, and start feeling good enough about yourself to have a little pep in your step. These things help you trust your own voice, but you have to go through the process to get there.

There's no one I respect more than my mom and dad. They've given everything they have to raise my brother and me to have a beautiful life. I was older when I came to the realization that everything they are was passed down to me. You may be thinking that's obvious, but think of it on a deeper level. The people who raised you transferred their own mindset, generational patterns, and beliefs to you, whether good or bad. However they were raised, whatever they saw or experienced as a kid that framed their thinking was passed on to you. Some things may have changed as they became adults and formed their own lifestyle and beliefs, but generally, our parents are developing us to the absolute best of their ability with what is familiar to them. Nobody is perfect, and no one can determine what's best for you except you. Over time (sometimes more quickly than others), you'll realize that your parents'/guardians' programming doesn't always agree with your own internal programming. You can take or leave whatever you want. The choice is yours. You can live life on your own terms or you can live off of somebody else's. When it's all said and done, you are the person who has to live with your choices. Choose wisely.

Growing into the person you want to become is uncomfortable. The feeling of doubt will often try to sneak in your life during transitional moments. Doubt will try to stifle your growth, and you'll wonder if you're doing anything right. This is where your support system shines. You become like the five people closest to you. Their habits will rub off on you and vice versa. Their sayings will rub off on you too. The way they challenge themselves, talk about themselves, and talk about other people will also drip onto you. You have to decide if you want other people's imprints on you, or if you want to avoid them like a pandemic. This choice isn't always easy. Sometimes, it'll cost you.

When I was in the process of seriously leveling up my life, my circle was supportive, but they were also always partying it up. We. We were always partying it up. I knew if I wanted to be all the things I'd been dreaming of, something had to change. I wanted to be positive, I wanted to feel good, and I wanted to build something that would change other people's lives, but I couldn't do that if I was working all week and curing hangovers on the weekend. I had to make the choice to change my friend group. I knew all the time it was worth it, but man, some days it was lonely. Sometimes I wondered if I was blowing things out of proportion. Was I too harsh? Too strong? But then God. God showed me more clarity and fulfillment in the areas I'd been praying about. I knew I'd done the right thing. Friendships and relationships go through stages, and I was moving into a different stage. I started to meet people who were going where I was going and learned the value of keeping a small circle of close friends and a larger outer ring of acquaintances. I became very careful about who was influencing my life, and since then, I've discovered it's a constant growth cycle.

Whatever you do, make sure you're not saying no to yourself when you say yes to letting someone in. Boundaries are your friend; people pleasing is not. Protect your peace and energy at all costs. Anybody who doesn't understand that is not inner circle material.

The key to transitioning in life is finding a way to enjoy every step of it. Although it's not always easy, staying very intentional with your happiness is crucial. When people are removed from your life, it creates space for friendships and relationships that were meant for you.

When it comes to all the things you're "supposed" to do to be successful, I often find myself on the outskirts. One of those things is finding a niche and staying in that space. For me, that just doesn't work.

I believe in chasing more than one dream at a time. For years people have told me, "Focus on one thing and become successful at that before you go to something else." I say no way Jose. Not everyone is built that way. I'm not made to work on just one thing. I am not functioning at my highest capacity when I'm focused on a single dream. For a person who operates this way, the name of the game is juggling, not balancing.

In high school, it was various sports and organizations. In college, it was class, pageantry, studying abroad, and nannying for a family with four amazing children. At that time, I was also president and co-founder of a retail organization in the business school. After college, it was outside sales, volunteering, and creating kids' sports drives. I'm a creator and a visionary. There's always something new to be done, and I love being the one to do it. That's evident in my business today, where I wear many different hats and thrive off of providing multiple services for my clients. I feel suffocated when people try to limit me and keep me in a box.

Even though I may be the best version of myself when I'm chasing many things at once, that doesn't mean you are too. The most wonderful thing about that is there is no right or wrong. It's your life and it is what you make of it. One of the most important things to keep in mind when you're creating the life of your dreams is to keep a healthy mindset, work out, and make time for family and friends. I don't say yes to everything. If my intuition is telling me there's something off, or if it doesn't align with my short- and long-term vision for myself, I say no. When you do the things that help you operate at your highest level, you'll know how to keep yourself happy and fulfilled.

Chapter 16

WHO INFLUENCES YOUR LIFE?

You become like the five people you surround yourself with most, and let me tell you, that statement has proven true in my life time and time again. Who you spend your time with is going to impact you, whether you intend it to or not. That's why you often see the athletes gravitate toward other athletes, the artists with the other creatives, the business owners with other business owners. You start to attract what you are, and the people you're around are who you become.

When I was in high school, I became good friends with a girl who unknowingly had a bit of sass to her, but she was fun to hang around. After a while, I realized she didn't show much respect toward her mother. One day, my mom called me into our laundry room (where all the serious conversations happened) to call me out on acting like this girl.

"Tori, you're starting to act like your new friend from school."

"No I'm not," I said, rolling my eyes.

"Yes you are, Tori. You know, you do start to act like whoever you're hanging out with, and I can tell your personality is starting to change."

"What do you mean, Mom? I'm my own person. I'm not acting like anyone else," I said, all mouthy. My mom and I have always been so close and rarely argued, but changes like this happen subconsciously. Before you know it, your personality and how you speak to others can shift.

Momma was right again, gosh darnit.

Years ago, I was hanging around a group of friends in a new city. I was training during pageant season, and you wouldn't catch me going off my nutrition plan. I figured I'd go out with my friends but be the designated driver. That way, I could hit my goals without missing out on the fun with my crew. We decided to go out one night, and while we were at a friend's house getting ready to leave, I noticed a few of the guys going into the bathroom one by one and coming out with newfound energy. They must be excited for the night, I thought as I grabbed my friend's car keys and took my place in the driver's seat.

During dinner, one of my friends excused himself to go to the bathroom. Our restaurant was a few stories up. I glanced out the window and saw my friend, who was "in the bathroom," outside the building secretly exchanging something with a man. I knew it was sketchy. I knew it had to do with drugs. And I knew I didn't want anything to do with it. I turned to my other friend sitting next to me and looked at her with the most perplexed expression. That's when she told me what was going on.

I was furious, knowing that I had just driven his car with God knows what in the backseat, and my "friend" hadn't said a word about it. I called a driver to take me home. I knew it was time to make some hard decisions.

When I called my friend the next day, I was nervous about how this was going to go down. I'd never had to "break up with a friend" before, but I knew it was necessary for my own well-being and future. This guy was truly my friend, and he had a good heart, but he'd gotten caught in a pattern of bad decision-making and gone down the wrong path. I didn't want my reputation damaged because I made the decision to stay friends with someone who didn't have a desire to change. You can't want something for someone more than they want it for themselves. I called him, explained that our choices and goals weren't aligning, wished him the best, and told him I hoped he stayed safe and that God blessed his future. That was when I took a detour from that group of friends.

You'll start to mirror your friends, whether you try to or not. You'll start to use the same lingo, make the same decisions, and pick up each other's habits. Be honest with yourself and decide if hanging out with your current circle is beneficial or detrimental to you. If it isn't a positive circle to be in, don't stick around and wait on them to change, because they probably won't—especially on your timing. If they're caught up in detrimental behaviors and don't think they need to change, that's their decision to make, but protecting yourself is your responsibility. Look around you. Who are your friends? Are they lifting you up or tearing you down? Are they good or bad influences on your life? I'm not asking if they're good people; most people have positive traits. There are tons of good people in the world, but that doesn't mean you need to hang out with all of them. I'm asking if their habits and behaviors are ones you'd be content owning yourself. Would you want people to describe you the way they describe your friends? Pay attention to their decisions, not their potential.

I'll never forget taking the leap from Iowa to Arizona to start over as the newfound Tori. The thing I prayed for the most during that time was to be surrounded by solid Christian friends. Even though I've been a Christian for as long as I can remember, I never really had friends I could pray with, probably because I wasn't taking the initiative either. Prayer and a solid support system became a huge focus for me once I realized God was the only one who could fully repair my confidence after my world flipped upside down.

I prayed that whatever God did in the next phase of my life in Arizona, he'd provide me with Christian friends who could build me up and hold me accountable to who I was becoming. In order to find these friends, I knew I needed to put myself in a position to attract what I was asking for, so my first week in Arizona, I joined a life group at a church I'd attended once before. I'd taken confirmation classes when I was younger, but had never been a part of a life group as an adult, so I had no idea what to expect. On the first night, the leader split us into two groups. I was intimidated. I love God. I love Jesus. But at this point, I was pretty insecure about my knowledge of Scripture. Additionally, I was still healing from my past relationship, so I was smiling of course, but my sadness was undeniable once I started talking. I was trying to put my life back together like a jigsaw puzzle, and here I was, about to spill my heart out in front of all these strangers. Lord help me.

We got into our groups, and our group leader, Shay, passed around a sheet of paper with instructions on how the rest of the evening was going to unfold. She explained further that we'd all go around in a circle and answer the question of the month, then tell everyone how we would like them to help us. Did I need advice, prayer, support, or just a listening ear? It was a vulnerable position to be in, but of course, as God's people, we all come together to encourage and support one another. Then she gave us the question:

How would you describe your last month in one word?

She had to be kidding. How could I put my last thirty-day debacle of uprooting my life into a single word? I'd just left the man I thought I'd be with forever, lost friends through the process, and had never been so emotionally broken in my entire life. My reality had been shattered by a sledgehammer, I was new in town after moving cross-country to rebuild, and now here I was, about to fall apart in a room full of strangers because of one simple question. I felt the urge to sprint out of there, but my tears moved quicker than my feet.

I couldn't fight it. I bawled my eyes out, right there in front of those people whose names I didn't know and whose faces I couldn't have picked out of a lineup. In the back of my mind, I thought, Well, you got what you wanted. You prayed for Christian friends. Here's a circle of believers giving you their full attention, and they're going to pour into you for a little while.

One thing about me: receiving hasn't always been my strong suit. I love advice from others, but when it comes time to have others pour love and support on me when I'm expressing my feelings, well, sometimes I don't know how to handle that. It hasn't always been easy for me to be vulnerable and show my weakness. I asked myself that question again, "How would you describe your last month in one word?"

"Challenging," I said, as I took a big gulp from the lump in my throat, my head down, crying. Shay proceeded to ask, "Would you like to talk about it more or would you just like prayer?" Whether I wanted to or not, my story flowed right out of me as I fought through the tears. They saw my grief and held space for me. Shay prayed over me. I knew right then that God had brought me to that moment.

God answered my prayers that day. I've continued to stay friends with many of the people in that group, and those friendships have led to other like-minded relationships in life and business. It feels good to be inspired by others who are on the same page as you and who challenge you to continuously learn and grow.

Had I stayed where I was, this couldn't have happened. When I stepped into the unknown and moved to Arizona, I was intentional about who I wanted to surround myself with. The purpose and promise that move brought me were unmatched. I had to leave my comfort zone, and I had to do it in pain, but I did it and quickly reaped the rewards.

It might seem a little direct when I say to be intentional about your friends, but you have to be a gatekeeper of what you let into your life. That goes for friendships, relationships, and the rooms you find yourself in. Pay attention to what and who you're attracting and who you let have influence over you, both in person and online. There's no need to put yourself in a position of unhealthy frequency. Pay attention to your triggers and lean in to figure out what internal work you need to do so you can heal. Once you have a circle of influence in place that directly correlates with the future you want, hold on tight to them. Even more importantly than that, make sure you're reciprocating the value they bring to you. It's a two-way street.

When I was younger, I didn't realize the importance of my circle, but every year it seems to have a bigger impact on my everyday life. It's a very simple concept: If your friends make bad decisions, you will too. If your friends make good decisions, you will too. If you hang out with people who party all the time, you'll party all the time. If your tribe is goal-oriented and focused, you'll set high goals as well. Your circle of influence directly correlates with your success. When you see you need to reanalyze your circle, the results will outweigh the discomfort of the moment. If your circle doesn't line up with the trajectory you want for your life, adjust. Take your life seriously. You only get one.

Chapter 17

OVERCOMING THE FEAR OF FAILURE

I know you know somebody who is super talented, full of phenomenal potential and great ideas, has the connections to make anything happen that they'd like, annnd then they don't. Why do people do this? Well, for all kinds of reasons. They don't have time. They don't have money. They don't have support. They don't know how to take the next step. But when they want to watch the latest binge-worthy series, they find time. When they want to treat themselves to a trip or fancy dinner, they find the money. When there isn't a shoulder to lean on, they become their own support. When they don't know how to work something, they find an online video to show them how. We've all been there. But the truth behind all of these excuses is one thing: fear.

Fear is an illusion that has the power of a brick wall. It'll keep you from living your greatest life. The only way is through it. What are talented, brilliant people afraid of? Scared to look like a fool in front of their peers, scared to take the chance on uncertainty, or even scared of success, like I was at one point. People oftentimes don't want to put forth all the effort and resources it takes to make something take off just for it to not work out. If they do that, they think they'll look like a failure and feel like one too. The fear of uncertainty can be treacherous.

Fear can paralyze you. It can paralyze you in the moment, or it can paralyze you for the long term and keep you stuck in thinking or planning mode until the years have flown past and you've still not accomplished anything. Think about things you've wanted to try, but didn't because you couldn't imagine you'd ever be able to get past what scared you.

Public speaking is one of the world's most common fears. Even people who love to do it still get nervous when it's time to hit the stage. It's normal to get a little shaky before you're in front of a room full of people who are there just to hear what you have to say. The reason we get intimidated (and this is the case in most situations) is because we are afraid of what others might think or say about us, especially if we value their opinions. A friend asked me how he could get rid of the fear of public speaking. "I know what I want to say; I just need to get past the fear part." Since I've spent a big chunk of my life on stage, I gave him my best advice.

When I was training to compete in Miss USA, I was super nervous about standing in front of a group of people who would be judging me mostly on external traits. It wouldn't have mattered who the judges were going to be; my heartrate was going to spike once I was behind the curtain no matter what. But you know who judges Miss USA? Celebrities.

Intimidation Level 10.

If you want to take care of business during a performance, you gotta practice in the same atmosphere, or as close to it as you can get. It was time to face my fears. Literally. I printed out the headshots of the five most intimidating people I could think of, went to the dance studio, taped the faces on the glass, and practiced in front of them. It worked! Of course, I was nervous on stage, but at that point it was pure excitement. When it was time to do my thing, I was able to because, again, I'd been there before. I'd put myself in the situation so when it came to game time, I wouldn't be surprised. It worked so well that I still do it today.

Look, if something is in your heart and it won't let you go, it's there for a reason. You need to act on it and figure out the path as you go along. Take the leap and just move! God will bless your path, but he rewards those who take action.

One day I had this brilliant idea that I'd try out for the dance team. Logistically, it would have been a nightmare. I was a starter on my basketball team playing all four quarters, and I was one of the leading scorers, but something inside of me was telling me to try out for the dance team as well. If it was meant to be, all the details would work themselves out. It all made sense to me, but my basketball coach was trying to figure out what the heck I was doing.

"When do you think you'll be able to dance?" he asked.

Excited about the possibility of doing something new and over-flowing with ideas, I replied, "I can play the first two quarters of the game, change into my dance uniform, dance during halftime, then change back before the third quarter starts so I can finish out the game."

"I don't see how that's going to work with you missing the half-time talks but do what you want," he said, laughing.

I didn't think much more of it. I was just pumped that I could do it all. I went to tell the dance instructor the same thing I'd told my coach, and she responded like he did but handed me a practice schedule anyway. I couldn't make it to either of the tryouts because I had basketball, but I didn't let that stop me. There's a way around everything, and I was going to figure out the way.

I asked her to send me the dance music and a video of the routine. Keep in mind, I'd never danced a day in my life. Matter of fact, I'd always been terrible at it. I didn't know any of the moves, and I had no idea how to even hold my hands. I had to learn all of this from the Internet. I was way past clueless. But I took the music and routine video and went to work in my front yard after basketball practice memorizing the moves, just me and my boombox. The two practices ended, and tryouts came along, which I couldn't make it to . . . because I had a basketball game. The dance coach told me to go ahead and send her a recorded video for my tryout if I felt so compelled, but she didn't see it happening. I forwarded her my video and waited.

The next week, they announced who'd made the team. My name was not on the list. I wasn't surprised, but I was pretty impressed how I'd convinced myself that I could juggle those two commitments in the first place!

I'm one of those people you would call "multipassionate," so I try it all. That thinking probably stems from my parents telling me I could do whatever I work hard enough for. People might think I'm all over the place, but you know what I never have to worry about? "What if." What if I'd have done this, what if I'd have tried that? If you don't try, you never know. It was like that with pageantry, it was like that with sports, it's like that with business, and it'll be like that many times in the future. You never know where your destiny lies; life is full of surprises. So if something sparks your interest, find out what that spark is about. When you hesitate, ask yourself what's holding you back. Get to the bottom of it, because if you don't figure it out, it may keep you from your bigger purpose. There's probably an idea that's popping up in your head right now—going for that new opportunity, moving across the country, taking an online course, changing career paths, trying a new hobby, going for that relationship—that's begging for your attention. If you ignore it, you're not only hindering yourself, you're also blocking all the people who would benefit from you doing what you're supposed to be doing.

You know, there's a time and place for everything in your life. The fear of failure can be crippling for some; for others, it may be the fear of success. Have you ever been scared of what your family or friends may think of you if you took a leap of faith and moved to a place more aligned with your goals and personality? Have you ever had thoughts of becoming so successful that your friends or family wouldn't be able to relate to you anymore? Are you afraid that you'll lose sight of what's most important in life? Maybe you're afraid that once you become successful, you'll have all the resources in the world to do whatever you want, but you won't know what to do with it all. Can I just help you with the first step? Be who you want to be with or without the success, and you'll become more of who you are when you get it. Now get out of your head and chase the heck after that dream. Stop overthinking it. Do it for you and not everyone else. Buckle up, enjoy the ride, and say peace out to fear!

Chapter 18

LET YOUR OBSESSION FLY

We love a good success story, don't we? Watching somebody emerge as a champion stirs up the belief that we can do great things, too. To see someone overcome the odds, dig deep, find it in themselves to pull through when they thought they were at their end, and then have all that grit pay off is so inspiring. People who have won before know what it takes and will never criticize you for starting once you begin your journey. Someone who has been in your shoes knows the struggle and respects the hustle. You can always tell the people who aren't winning; they're busy criticizing someone else's starting point. The truth of the matter is winners lose more than they win. That's how they figure out what it takes to become a champion.

I believe it's a lifelong process of overcoming obstacles. It's the case for almost everybody. Hourlong documentaries can't fully capture the process of evolving from average to great, but understand that anyone who's worked for their success knows what it's like to fail. They use the lessons they gain from their losses to build a strong foundation. I would rather take ten years learning, growing, researching, and figuring out the best structure for a business instead of taking one year to try and scale something without establishing its foundation. A quick strategy isn't always the best strategy. The point of winning and losing is to establish that strong foundation, not only for the game you're trying to win, but also for your character. While winning is certainly more fun, losing teaches you valuable lessons that winning can't. Let's take a look at the benefits of hearing "no."

HUMILITY

It may seem obvious, but not succeeding at something shows you that you're not the best. It forces you to reflect, pinpoint your weaknesses, and tackle them each day as you work to overcome them. Losing lets you know that you haven't already arrived at your dream destination, which can be extremely humbling. When you put in the work, you prove to yourself that you can overcome failure, you get noticed, and all of that combined grows your confidence.

EMPATHY

When you've felt the pain of second best, you naturally become a little more empathetic toward others when they walk a similar path. Think about it: who wants a leader who can't relate to the feelings they're experiencing?

PERSEVERANCE

Defeat does not feel good, but perseverance makes you feel invincible! The adrenaline of getting back up when you've been knocked down beats the valley of defeat. Perseverance isn't for the faint of heart. You need to have a "team meeting" with yourself and push through the bully in your head trying to tell you that you can't do it. When you feel like quitting, push in further. That's when you discover your limits, which are always farther than you thought.

RESTRUCTURING

Winning is not just about talent; it's also about strategy. Losing forces you to think through the processes you've been using so you can figure out what to keep and what to throw out the window. Reworking your goals and the steps you'll take to reach them is the blueprint of a champion. You can't keep doing what you've been doing and expect something different.

Most of the time, your first time doing something isn't going to end with a big golden medal. It isn't supposed to. You haven't put in the work. Overnight successes and "naturals" are not the norm. If you ever try achieving something noteworthy in this life, you might as well face the hard truth that you're more than likely going to lose first before you win. Once I started directing my focus more on enjoying the process instead of the pain of failure, my personal mantra became, "Every no is one step closer to my yes." I said it in pageantry, I say it in my personal life, and now I say it in business. When somebody says no, look at it as an opportunity to learn, not a reason to throw yourself a pity party and recruit all your friends to join you. Don't give energy to the feeling of losing. Instead, reframe it and show gratitude for the loss. Say, "Thank you for that no, because now I'm just one step closer to my yes." Then, reanalyze what you need to do to get your yes.

I learned how to reanalyze through basketball. When I reflected on a game or watched film with my team, I could see what I did well and where I needed to improve. If I didn't catch a mistake, my coach would yell, "KRUSER!" to make sure it didn't go unnoticed for another second. I could also see whether I gave it my all, and honestly, the answer to that question wasn't always yes. Not getting that "W" you wanted forces you to figure out your identity. Too often, our worth can get wrapped up in activities and achievements and whether we're winning or losing. Instead, try placing your identity in your faith and who you are as a person, not accolades and awards. If you fail, cry it out, get back up, and focus on an area of improvement for the next time. I was told no so many times in pageantry, I could write a book just about that. Even now, as I continue to build my business, people tell me no every day. Instead of feeling hurt or angry, I'm grateful for another day of growth. This isn't always an easy mindset to stay in. In fact, I've learned life will always give you tests to see if you'll stay strong. However, you can't lose when you put your focus on gratitude for the situation. Everything is happening for you.

A few years ago I created my first digital course and group coaching program. I'd planned for fifteen participants, marketed to hundreds, and put in long hours while other people were sleeping to curate a course that would give my clients unbeatable value.

I got to work writing an outline, writing scripts, setting up my home studio, shooting videos, editing, and editing some more until I felt like the course was perfect. With high hopes, I reached out to about two hundred girls on social media. I sent customized individual messages with video and everything. Were they interested? Yes. Were they excited? Very! Were they signing up? Nah. No biggie—I just viewed every no as taking one step closer to the one yes that would multiply into fifteen yesses, but in the end, the math didn't add up.

The day before launch, when I was busting my tail to get girls signed up for the program, I texted my brother and asked, "Dude, if you had one person in your program right now and it started in five hours, what would you do?" He replied, "I would act like there were thirty people." A bolt of energy shot through me as I laughed at our shared tenacity, but he'd read the question wrong. What I really wanted to know was what practical marketing steps he would take to get more people signed up. He replied, "Well, that's your expertise. You know that the best!"

You see, we don't always see our own talents. Sometimes it takes the people closest to us to remind us of who we are. He was right. I'd been in their shoes. I'd had their same feelings and struggles. I knew what social platforms they were on, and I knew exactly what they needed. Why the heck was I doubting myself? Ask yourself the same question. Why are you doubting yourself in your own expertise? In what area are you asking other people for advice, but you already know the answer? You just need to do the work and get out of your own head.

It didn't seem cost- or time-effective to follow through with the launch date because when it came time, I only had ONE person registered. Then I remembered all I'd been taught about showing up, put on my winning smile, and ran that first video call. I gave all I could considering the circumstances, but things just got worse. My one participant logged off in the middle of the call. I felt like a clown sitting there, talking to myself. But I'd done only half of what I'd committed to do. I'd shown up. Now I just had to finish strong.

When it was over, and I was completely deflated, I checked my email. I just knew that my one participant was going to email me and ask for a refund. Where had I gone wrong? Do you know how frustrating it is to know you have what other people need right there in your hands, and you offer it to them, but nobody bites? It's brutal, my friend. Brutal.

They say when you're in a competition and everything is going right, you don't get tired. Had people told me yes and shown up for that first session, I'd have gotten off that call feeling like I could have run a marathon. But they didn't, so when I hung up with my one client, I felt like the whole world had just seen me fail. At that point, I had a choice. I could pout in my sorrow, or I could boss up. I felt sorry for myself for a few minutes, then I picked my head up. "Tori, be proud of yourself. You didn't quit."

Customers in this specific industry were spending their money somewhere—I just needed to figure out how to get them to spend it with me. After simmering in disbelief for a few minutes, with the video call window still on my screen, I decided to write about what I was feeling right in that moment. I needed some clarity and perspective.

During the process of questioning what I'd done right and wrong, I remembered some important truths. If I was doing what I felt called to do, I needed to trust that I was where God needed me to be at the time. Zechariah 4:10 tells us not to despise the day of small beginnings. Even if you're beginning again. Even if it's in a realm you thought you'd already mastered.

My dad has always said, "Life is a learning experience." When things don't go your way, even though you did everything you were supposed to do, you cannot give up. You can be disappointed, but don't sit in discouragement. Refuse to believe that one failure is the sum of your worth. This concept is the same in every area of your life. A "no" isn't the end unless you say it is. It might be the end of a job, relationship, or whatever else you have going on, but if you can walk away from that one thing knowing you did all you could do, that knowledge frees you up to strut right into the next thing, using the prior experience as fuel for future success. Cry your tears and give yourself some time to be sad before you blow the dust off your pen and start planning a new course of action.

Winners fail the most. They even fail after they win. You might witness their huge success and put them on a pedestal, but afterwards, they turn around, go home, try something, and fail again more than others will ever know. Success isn't handed to us. I truly believe knowing how to fail and get back up is a skill set we don't address enough. While failures might seem like they're taking over your life at the time, what defines you is how you recover. The only way forward is through self-reflection, adjustment, and massive action.

Grant Cardone says you can be obsessed or you can be average. If you're not built for average, it's time to let your obsession fly.

You have to shield your brain against getting stuck. We have everything we need inside of us to grab the success we desire so much, but we get scared, lose focus, and get flustered when everything doesn't go as planned the first time. I know I can achieve anything I put my mind to, and I know this because I've proven it to myself before. You have, too. Just think about anything you had to learn to do—tie your shoes, ride your bike without training wheels, put on makeup, play an instrument, learn to dance, play soccer, or twist your spaghetti onto your fork. In your life, you've perfected something. You've done it once, and you can do it again. Stop being so hard on yourself.

You'll see a lot of losses along the way. All those losses can knock your confidence down to nothing. When this happens, it's time to let that childlike belief take over. Kids don't hang on to failures for long. They get up, brush the grass off their knees, and keep going because they don't know they're not supposed to. Whatever mental blocks your mind tries to convince you of, kick them down. They don't belong there. Our God of the Universe has a much bigger plan for you. Getting there will be all the things—frustrating, beautiful, time-consuming, fulfilling, deflating, and empowering. That's life. You have to learn to take the good with the bad, or better yet, stop categorizing things as good or bad; just see them for what they are, and be grateful for the variety of experiences that life provides.

Chapter 19

BE THE UNEXPECTED

Do you remember your first legit roller coaster ride? With the obnoxious twists and turns and dips? You made it through those and had just caught your breath when suddenly you felt like you might fly out your seat, then you dropped back down so quickly your stomach was in your throat? That's entrepreneurship, in all its glory.

My first year of business had major highs and lows. It was like throwing ideas of taffy on the wall just to see what would stick. Finally, in year two, the ball started to roll, but the pressure was mounting. I was trying to discover what my next keynote was going to be about. I was doing what I'd always known I would, which was speaking on stages and sharing my experiences to positively influence others, but I needed to be sure I was leading the audience in the right direction. I would often get in my own head when I looked at other people in the speaking and coaching industry and convince myself they had it all figured out. Why do we do that?! People, NOBODY HAS IT ALL

FIGURED OUT! Some have more puzzle pieces in place than others, but no one's puzzle is complete. Plus, at any moment, someone could bump the table and throw all those puzzle pieces across the floor. I needed to get a handle on my thoughts, so I called my friend Emily. When you're in doubt, scared, or need clarity, call a friend who knows you best and sees you in a different light from how your family sees you or how you see yourself.

"How would you describe me?" I asked her.

She thought about it for a few seconds before she replied, "Completely unexpected."

I can't lie, I thought her answer was pretty cool. I needed some details, and if I'm keeping it real with you, a confidence boost.

"Tell me more," I said.

Emily talked about how she wouldn't expect a pageant girl to also be "real" and not egotistical. She didn't expect me to have a tomboyish side that's super sarcastic, or to be someone who can joke around one minute and be professional the next. She said everything about me is unexpected. I learned a lot of lessons through that conversation.

Me being me, I was ready to hit the ground running with this new revelation. We brainstormed for hours. If you're stumped, in a funk, or questioning the path you need to take, or if you don't have a coach or mentor but you need some immediate insight, bouncing ideas around with someone you love and trust is a goldmine. People closest to you can see from the outside what you can't from the inside.

Emily proceeded to tell me that I could really build on this idea. We brainstormed about how to be close with your family but a strong business woman, how to have strong faith but also be a lot of fun, and how to keep humility and confidence in all areas of your life.

I never would have thought of that on my own. Everyone needs an Emily in their life. While the world is programmed to judge you based on external traits and accolades, be the one who starts showing up in unexpected ways. Be the light the world really needs.

I want to ask you a question, and I want you to dig deep before you answer. The life you're living now, is it based on who you really are, or is it based on other people's perceptions of you? Are you shrinking to fit into somebody else's mold, or are you unapologetically yourself? How are you showing up in unexpected ways in your life? What beliefs and opinions are people putting on you that you're allowing to flow into your routine, your mind, your emotions, and your outcomes? If that's happening, this is your permission to put an end to it. Be the real you, despite what others say or perceive.

In order to journey through this transformation within, sometimes we have to embrace the battle. It isn't fun or easy, but you have to find a way to do it to reach the peak of the space you want to excel in. Dig into the lessons your hard times taught you. Make peace with your past hurt. Forgive yourself for what you didn't know. Show yourself some grace. When you do that, you can build a foundation that won't collapse when storms come.

Nothing sustainable will happen overnight. Skyscrapers will fall at the first strike of a tornadic wind if their foundations aren't deep. Your goals can be gigantic, but if you rush through them too quickly and inefficiently, you'll miss some important lessons along the way. Something about what you're trying to build needs to be built on some essential, already existing groundwork. When you start laying the bricks, they need to align with the foundation. Embrace those building blocks.

When I started entrepreneurship, I already had experience in overcoming obstacles, embracing individualized competition, and consistent family support. Your foundation doesn't have to be prior work experience, a degree, or all the knowledge possible about a topic, but it needs to relate in some way to what you're striving for, and it needs to be stormproof. When you prepare intentionally, you'll always have a truth, a concept, or an experience to hold on to when nothing seems to be working to assure you that you're on the right track and you have what it takes to make it.

When you're performing the life everyone expects of you, it's hard to make the tough decisions that you'll need to make to keep going. But man, performing that expected life is easy. People will be so proud of you, and you won't challenge them at all—but you'll be dying inside trying to keep everyone else happy. It would have been so easy to stay at the flooring sales job I had after college. It was safe, it was comfortable, I worked with amazing people, and I had great benefits. Isn't that the American Dream? I could have made a great living there, raised a family there, and had a life others would call successful. But it wasn't what God had put in my heart. No one expected me to quit that job to go to LA and pursue modeling and TV hosting. I didn't even see that coming! My internal feelings were saying to stay in the safe zone, but I knew that was just fear of the unknown coming back up. Think of all the opportunities and life experiences that wouldn't have happened if I'd listened to that fear. I wouldn't have understood the power of stepping outside my comfort zone and into the unknown like I do now. I most likely wouldn't have become a speaker, written this book, or owned my company, all by the time I was thirty years old. Learn to tell the difference between the two voices in your head: the one holding you back and the one telling you to have faith and believe in the process. Go with faith and take massive action along with it. Just in case you missed that part—Faith! Plus! Action! It's GO TIME!

Chapter 20

DO IT FOR YOU

I've learned many lessons from this journey of ups and downs and noes to yesses, but one thing is consistent: if you don't do it for yourself, no one will do it for you.

Yes, I've taken the uncertain route many times. But I've also talked myself out of opportunities because I was focused on what people would think of me. A great way to undo that conditioning is to do something daily that your future self will thank you for. As you go about living in the present, consider how your decisions today will influence tomorrow. Then do it with everything you've got. When you do what makes you feel alive, it's an instant happy pill. When you're happy, you have more respect for yourself and your time. You start showing up better for yourself, and you begin to show up better for others as well. You start saying yes to the right people and opportunities and no to the people and things that don't align with your calling. You do them from the overflow of joy within you, not from resentful obligation and exhaustion. That, my friend, is how the world gets the best benefit from your gifts. It's also how you honor your work while honoring yourself.

If you struggle with setting healthy boundaries—and most of us have at some point in our lives—begin by blocking out time for yourself on your calendar like you schedule everything else. Schedule time for your mental health, your workout, your spa time, your friend time—whatever brings you joy—and make it a non-negotiable. I was talking to a friend who was telling me how many things she had on her to-do list, but she didn't have time for self-care. I told her to set the time in her schedule and not to budge on it. She seemed confused. She asked me, "Well, what if someone wants to talk with me at the time I set aside for myself? So I gave her a tip. I told her to use that little powerful two-letter word. In our culture, we think telling someone "no" is offensive. We need to change that perception. If you don't look after you, you better believe no one else will. You'll set the precedent for endless availability, so that will be people's expectation of you. You will work yourself to sickness or burnout. As long as you give, others will take. They might not mean it to hurt you, but you will pay the price. Say yes to yourself consistently. People should not have unlimited access to you. Thank me later.

What are you going to do with that personal time? Again, whatever makes you happy. If you've been going so hard that you don't even know what you like anymore, hooray for self-discovery! When you are happy, that happiness trickles into every area of your life, and I'm telling you, being happy in your work is the absolute best way to serve others. Have you ever done anything you absolutely hated? Have you ever watched someone go to a job that was slowly sucking the life out of them, but they went because they felt like they had to? Take a second and think about what that's like. Now, have you ever watched someone do something with pure bliss? It doesn't matter what it was. I've watched custodians sweep floors and sprinkle joy all over the hallways. I've watched rested moms run circles around everybody at the park with their children. I've also seen CEOs collect big checks and hate life, and moms who'd give anything for just thirty minutes of silence and to listen to their favorite songs on repeat. When you look after yourself, you're doing it for the people around you as much as you're doing it for you.

Friend, God didn't give you another day because you needed it; he gave you another day because someone needs you. Think of the impact you could have with a foundation of love, joy, purpose, excitement, and the skills to turn challenges into triumphs. This isn't just about you. That's why it's not selfish as we know the word "selfish." When you take care of yourself, you're in a position to give your best. When you work or give to others from the overflow of joy in your heart, others benefit. But that can't happen if you don't look out for yourself first. When you engage in self-care, only then can you serve the world at your highest capacity. That's what fulfillment is.

When I'm in a funk of any sort, I start giving. The lessons you gain through this life are to be shared. If you see a fun workout at the gym, listen to a great podcast, or find an inspiring personal development book, but you keep it all to yourself, what's the point? Those are all tools to help you show up best in the world, not to keep a secret. If you hear something that enhances your life, share it. If you read something that gives you valuable insight, tell somebody. Whenever you come across something that can inspire someone else, spread it. There's enough to go around. Awesomeness multiplies.

As you're planning and preparing to level up your life, there will be times when you're scared. Terrified actually. I still get butterflies in my stomach when I'm about to speak on a stage in front of an audience. When that happens, or when I'm fearful for any reason, I remind myself that I'm focusing too much on myself and I need to look outwards. If what I'm about to do or say will positively impact just one person, then I'm going to give it my all. I can't let fear get in the way. Look at yourself as a vessel. Don't worry about if they'll like you, if you're going to mess up, or any other limiting beliefs. Flip the script and believe that because of the leap of faith you're about to take, you're going to bless someone's life. Every day, someone needs your love, light, talent, and gifts. It could be at the gas station or the coffee shop; it doesn't have to be on a big stage. You are needed right where you are.

What most people don't know is that for many years, before I'd go on stage for pageants, my knees would shake uncontrollably as I stood behind the curtain in my six-inch heels. I'd put so much pressure on myself to give it my all that I felt nervous to my core, but I remember telling myself, "Tori, do it for the girls at home who aren't able to be on this stage right now." My knees would slowly stop shaking. It wasn't about me anymore. I focused on passing this gift on and doing it for a bigger purpose. I use the same tactic now for speaking. My message could give someone in the audience the exact courage they need to make a major life change. I don't say this to be egotistical, I say this because you have the same power within you. You never know how your words and actions are going to speak to someone that day. Show up in the world and spread your gift.

Your future is in your hands. What will you do with it? Think about that as you're planning your day. Every decision you make today is trickling into your future. Is it holding you back or setting the stage for breakthrough? Having trouble finding your motivation? Here it is:

Everything you desire is on the other side of your comfort zone, and you have the power to create it. Go get it. Chase after it fearlessly. Pursue the career. Get out of the relationship that's holding you back.

Sign up for the health plan and achieve the body of your dreams. Take that trip. Move across the country. Do the thing that you've been scared to do. All things are possible. Stop settling for mediocrity or listening to the bully inside of your own head that's telling you you can't, because you can. If you're scared of the spotlight or what people will think of you, consider if that fear is worth your peace. Don't settle because it makes someone else comfortable. Only listen to God and your gut. Your intuition is always right—trust it! You are special. You are unique. God made you the way you are for a reason, so embrace it.

Tomorrow is not promised; all we have is the present moment. All of your experiences have shaped who you are and who you're becoming. It's time to start thinking bigger than ever before. Stop making excuses, and just go do the dang thing! Find the people who have your back, and make sure you have theirs. Take action every day, move your body, eat something healthy, pray like your life depends on it (because it does), and take the next steps toward the life that's waiting for you on the other side. Do it for the people who need your beautiful light, energy, and everything you have to offer this world. But before you do it for others, you have to do it for you.

It's your time to shine. I believe in you!

References

[1] "Brain Architecture." *Harvard University: Center on the Developing Child.* https://developingchild.harvard.edu/science/key-concepts/brain-architecture/

[2] "Toxic Stress." *Harvard University: Center on the Developing Child.* https://developingchild.harvard.edu/science/key-concepts/toxic-stress/

[3] Kendra Cherry. "Does Practice Really Make Perfect?" *VeryWell Mind.* Updated 21 Oct. 2020. https://www.verywellmind.com/does-practice-really-make-perfect-2795158

[4] Reviewed by Tyler Wheeler. "Why Sitting Too Much Is Bad for Your Health." *Jump Start by WebMD.* 25 Jan. 2022. https://www.webmd.com/fitness-exercise/ss/slideshow-sitting-health

[5] Kimberly Zapata. "How to Manifest Anything You Want or Desire." *Oprah Daily.* 22 Dec. 2020. https://www.oprahdaily.com/life/a30244004/how-to-manifest-anything/

[6] A.J. Adams, MAPP. "Seeing Is Believing: The Power of Visualization." *Psychology Today.* 3 Dec. 2009. https://www.psychologytoday.com/us/blog/flourish/200912/seeing-is-believing-the-power-visualization